GULLIVER UNBOUND

GULLIVER UNBOUND

America's Imperial Temptation and the War in Iraq

Stanley Hoffmann

with Frédéric Bozo

ROWMAN & LITTLEFIELD PUBLISHERS, INC.

Lanham • Boulder • New York • Toronto • Oxford

ROWMAN & LITTLEFIELD PUBLISHERS, INC.

Published in the United States of America
by Rowman & Littlefield Publishers, Inc.
A wholly owned subsidiary of
The Rowman & Littlefield Publishing Group, Inc.
4501 Forbes Boulevard, Suite 200, Lanham, MD 20706
www.rowmanlittlefield.com

P.O. Box 317, Oxford OX2 9RU, UK

Distributed by NATIONAL BOOK NETWORK

British Library Cataloguing in Publication Information Available

Library of Congress Cataloging-in-Publication Data Available

ISBN: 0-7425-3600-9

Printed in the United States of America

∞™ The paper used in this publication meets the minimum requirements of American National Standard for Information Sciences—Permanence of Paper for Printed Library Materials, ANSI/NISO Z39.48-1992.

CONTENTS

PREFACE

Even if my trajectory has brought me from the Institute of Political Sciences in Paris to Harvard, where I have been teaching for almost fifty years, I am not a "classical American professor." I am not embarrassed at having become a citizen of the United States, but it has to be clear that having been born in Vienna and then entirely educated in France, where I have received a schooling to which I owe being what I am, I have remained French. My relations with France are intense, as are relations of the heart and the mind. My best friends are in France and some became my friends in coming to Harvard to study.

I have written elsewhere that the administrative and social organization of France had forced me into a kind of exile. I had perhaps hoped that this heavy armor would get softer and make it possible for me to return. This has not happened, or at least not sufficiently. Nevertheless, I have resigned myself to an ambiguous condition: someone whom his nature, his choices, and his fate have made marginal in almost all possible ways, neither fully integrated in an America which, except for New England, remains largely unknown to me but not belonging either really to a France whose daily life I have not shared for many years. France is and will remain an essential part of my identity but it is not the only one. Like so many who came to the U.S., I am deeply attracted by many of America's features and strengths, and I also see myself as a cosmopolitan. As a liberal, I found my two nationalities highly compatible and I still do, despite the recent tensions.

This background explains perhaps why I have wanted to express my views on events that could not leave me indifferent, not only because they forced me to ask myself questions about America, but also because they affected me deeply, more than any previous Franco-American crisis, as a Frenchman and an American.

I have therefore accepted with great pleasure the idea of this book of conversations with my French friend and former student at Harvard, the historian Frédéric Bozo. The idea was suggested to us by Caroline Leclerc, also a former student at Harvard, who has become a publisher. These conversations took place at the end of June 2003, and the text was considerably revised during the summer of 2003. I knew that we were not always in agreement. Having talked with him during the events in Iraq, I knew that Frédéric Bozo was more skeptical than I concerning the French position versus the U.S. Perhaps our respective situations, with him in Paris and me in Cambridge, Mass., explain in part this contrast. But this difference only made the exercise more stimulating and the choice of the interview form allowed more informal and emotional exchanges than do academic books. The book was considerably augmented in the spring and summer of 2004, this time by myself alone. It thus takes into account the events of the fall, winter, and spring following the American occupation of Iraq.

GULLIVER
UNBOUND

1

THE FRANCO-AMERICAN CONFLICT

Bozo: Because of its regional and global dimensions, the Iraqi affair has been the occasion of one more transatlantic crisis, which was largely Franco-American. We have lived since the fifties through a large number of those episodes of tension between the U.S. and Europe and in particular between France and the U.S.: the European Defense Community, Suez, NATO, etc. How do you see the Iraqi crisis in the long succession of such events?

Hoffmann: I have lived in the United States for forty-nine years, and I have known many Franco-American crises. There was Suez in 1956, when Paris and London secretly conferred and then launched, in collusion with Israel, an intervention against Egypt which scandalized the Eisenhower administration. The situation was in many respects the opposite from this recent crisis; then, the impetuous powers were France and Great Britain and resistance came from Washington. But in the current case it was the United States that favored the path to war. Then there were very tough crises during the presidency of General de Gaulle. Americans did not like the general—it is the least one could say—but did at bottom respect him. De Gaulle "poisoned" the alliance but they had to take him into account; his rhetoric, his opposition to the war in Vietnam, irritated them considerably, his policy regarding Quebec and also his decision to withdraw from the military organization of NATO shocked the Americans, but they had a certain tolerance for him. He was wrong, they thought, but he had "the right to think what he wants." Indeed, Lyndon Johnson, whose foreign policy was more subtle than many have said, tried to avoid opposing himself systematically to de Gaulle so as not to further increase the general's international prestige. The Atlantic Alliance remained fundamental: in the eyes of the Americans NATO would not disappear simply because France withdrew from the integrated military structure but remained in the alliance. Then, as the war in Vietnam became more and more disastrous, the Americans understood that it was not malevolence, which explained why de Gaulle, ever since 1964, had tried to persuade them to find a compromise solution. They themselves understood that they could not go too far in their war in Vietnam so that no pretext could be used by the Chinese for getting more deeply involved in the conflict. They did not want to repeat the experience of Korea when Chinese "volunteers" intervened at their expense and they hoped that the Russians would pressure the North Vietnamese for a compromise. So that despite all their difficulties with de Gaulle, when France was hit by a financial crisis after the events of 1968, the Americans without any hesitation helped France. In 2003 this would have been inconceivable.

What was new about George W. Bush was the following "philosophy": to punish those who did not want to follow the

U.S., and the idea that Americans were so much stronger that others have to respect it and follow it. This notion had not existed under Bill Clinton nor under George Bush the First, a man who had a long and good international experience, nor had it been the case of their predecessors. Richard Nixon had been an admirer of the general; Henry Kissinger had a certain esteem for France. Throughout the Iraqi crisis, one had the impression, as the American diplomat Brady Kiesling said after he resigned from his post in Greece following twenty-five years in the American diplomatic service, especially in the Middle East, that the present American leaders were "barbarians" with no idea of what the external world was like.

Bozo: Given your personal itinerary and your condition as a Franco-American academic and intellectual, how have you personally lived through this crisis? Have you had disagreeable experiences?

Hoffmann: Contrary to what has happened in the past, what particularly shocked me in the crisis of 2003 was the extraordinarily contemptuous attitude of Americans: the White House, of course, but also the media, who were equally humiliating. This atmosphere was extremely difficult to live with. The argument was: "you are weak, therefore you are obliged to follow us because we Americans are always right, and when we decide that our national interest is at stake you cannot oppose us, and if you do not follow us, it is because you are not truly our ally." What was most shocking for Washington, it seems, was the spectacle of France looking for support among the United Nations, at a time when the Americans were doing exactly the same thing.

For me this period has been extremely painful in many respects. First, I expected a much stronger reaction, both in academic circles and in the media; but these milieus reacted with extraordinary weakness when they were not indeed depressingly subservient to the government. In trying to understand a little better what was happening behind the façade, I was horrified both by the cynicism and by the systematic exploitation of all the prejudices against France. I am not saying that everything was dictated by the White House, but the White House could have, from time to time, moderated the journalists by explaining to them that France, after all, was not Saddam Hussein. Journalists did not try to understand the French position.

I have also been surprised by the weak reaction from the French side. While the anti-Americanism of French intellectuals, which certainly was not new, surged again—of course this didn't help relations with Washington—French officials did not react with as much vigor as I thought was necessary. The French government behaved as if one was still in the days of secret diplomacy. This was probably because of the laudable concern not to provoke a bitter and angry quarrel with the American ally, but it took time to understand that with this new America it was necessary to resort to public relations: the British have always understood this, the French much less. It is true that the press and television have been much more reluctant to welcome the representatives of Jacques Chirac than those of Tony Blair. The remarkable French ambassador to Washington, Jean-David Levitte, sent many letters to the leading newspapers, which never published them. But it was only after the war itself was over that he went through the U.S. in order to explain and defend the French position. It was a bit late. The combative de Gaulle never waited.

Bozo: How do you explain this American francophobia, a phenomenon which is not new, but which many French people have discovered during this crisis? What are its genealogy and its successive layers? Should one go back to FDR and to his disappointment with France after its defeat in 1940? Or is it simply the price one has to pay for the challenges that de Gaulle and his successors addressed to the United States?

Hoffmann: American francophobia is an old and complicated phenomenon. It results from ancient stereotypes (the cynical and amoral French) and from historical events (for instance, France's refusal to reimburse its debts to the U.S. after the First World War). It is true that Roosevelt never forgave France for its defeat in 1940 and henceforth ceased to treat France as a great power, hence he had bad relations with de Gaulle. Later, at the time of the Fourth Republic, American elites displayed a mix of disdain and pity toward France because of its weak institutions, the slowness of reconstruction, the obstinacy of its colonialism, and the international impotence of the regime. There are still traces of this period in American analyses; I'm thinking of the columns of Thomas Friedman of the *New York Times*, which described France as a country incapable of modernizing itself, a country which missed the turn to globalization, and which is anti-American because it is blind to the advantages of globalization, i.e., the Americanization of the world. And then of course in the 1960s there was this mix of admiration and exasperation toward de Gaulle, which has left obvious traces. These layers have been somewhat forgotten. It is as if successive strata of resentment or contempt for France had surged again with the Iraq crisis.

Nevertheless the phenomenon is difficult to measure because, as is usual with polls, it all depends on the question. If the question had been, "Do you have the impression that France has betrayed us as an ally?", the answer would have been "Yes" by a huge majority. But if one had formulated the question differently: "Do you believe that from now on France should be excluded from American policy and only Britain or Poland should be listened to," much of the public would have answered with a shrug. As for the future, given the suddenness of the crisis and the fact that it is not over, it is uncertain but there probably will be traces for a long time and there will be more confrontation.

Bozo: Isn't there also a factor that is often neglected: the absence of a French minority in the U.S. (unlike in the case of Germany) and therefore the lack of a French presence in American society and the absence of any inhibition in the criticism of the French, as if the worst stereotypes were politically correct?

Hoffmann: It is true that Americans have gone much farther in Gallophobia than in Germanophobia, partly because there are millions of Americans of German origin, but let us not forget that Germany has no veto in the Security Council, unlike France, and remains reluctant to place itself in front, and thus exposes itself less than France.

Bozo: One also has the impression that the Germans have been somewhat spared by the fact that they adopted a position of principle, a pacifism that was open to criticism but honorable, whereas the position of the French, who are not known for their pacifism, has been interpreted as motivated by a systematic hostility toward the U.S, and by more or less shady interests.

Hoffmann: Indeed! French economic interests in Iraq have been exaggerated and denounced. But let us remember that, at the end of the summer of 2002, when Chancellor Schröder announced German opposition to the war, he was not greeted any better. The American government saw in it an internal maneuver chosen for purely electoral reasons, as if nothing of the kind ever happened in the U.S.! Television and radio have fed those criticisms: "Don't the Germans understand the absurdity of their position and the harm it causes to the allies?" But these reactions faded rather quickly and France became the scapegoat because the Security Council became the primary battlefield. Also, the whole background of quarrels with France, seen as an irretrievably anti-American country, reappeared. In the U.S. the necessary distinctions were not made between the old anti-Americanism of left-wing or right-wing intellectuals, what I have called the "anti-Americanism of state," which was de Gaulle's and targeted the weight of the U.S. in the world but not American culture or society, and criticism of the tough unilateralism of the Bush team presented (rather moderately in my opinion) by de Villepin. Gallophobia regrettably amalgamated these three very different kinds.

Bozo: To come to an end of this point, what in this wave of Gallophobia was sincere or genuinely passionate, and what was pure political calculation? Wasn't it, for the American administration, a way—certainly not a very elegant one—of exerting pressure on French diplomacy? Didn't it in fact work: after the end of America's military operations, didn't Chirac and de Villepin put some water into their wine?

Hoffmann: It is true that for American officialdom the desire to "punish" France resulted from a calculation. The United States needed a test case and France was an ideal target because it was a secondary power compared to Russia, but one whose ambition remains worldwide, contrary to Germany. Opinion followed. The purpose was to put France back in its place and to deter other countries from following its example, whereas one wanted to safeguard relations with Russia and, if possible, drive a wedge between Berlin and Paris.

Bozo: Let us ask some questions about French policy and its responsibilities in this Franco-American crisis. Aren't there wrongs on both sides? Haven't the old anti-American reflexes that you mentioned weighed on the French government's attitude and driven our leaders to confrontation, either out of conviction, almost unconsciously, or in order to be aligned with public opinion, i.e., consciously? In any case, didn't the French know how to analyze American policy and its roots? In a word, have they understood the extent to which the United States had changed after September 11?

Hoffmann: I have been deeply struck in discussions with Parisian friends by the fact that they have not perceived that what had happened was a kind of revolution. One had to be in the U.S. to understand this. French diplomats in the United States, despite their great qualities, were sometimes deeply circumscribed by Washington's atmosphere, attached to their daily work and not fully aware of the newness of the context, of the revolution in American strategy and of the fact that, in order to resist it, it was necessary to explain clearly and incessantly the French position, if only to oblige those who presented France as the defender of Saddam Hussein to shut up.

Bozo: Whatever reasons for this misreading, one has the impression that the French had wanted to see in the Iraqi affair a new "peripheral" crisis, as there had already been many (for instance, Vietnam), a crisis which did not concern America's vital interests and thus allowed for a posture of dissent or even opposition, whereas it was exactly the opposite for Washington, since as the Americans put it, the Iraqi affair concerned essential interests.

Hoffmann: I think there were on the French side two errors of appreciation. The first consisted in underestimating the worldwide importance of the war against terrorism in official American policy, and the second consisted in not understanding how much the assimilation of Iraq to terrorism had become the heart of the American government's position. After all, an average Frenchman or even an average Englishman didn't find this link obvious. But the Americans used the formula, "Iraq equals terrorism," in order to create a kind of obligation of loyalty for the allies. Even if one rejected this equation, the French underestimated the extraordinary exploitation of fear which the American administration fostered through repeated alarms, warnings, and rumors. I think that this may have been rather misunderstood on the French side. This error was possibly aggravated in the fall of 2002 by the vacuum in the French embassy in Washington between the departure of Ambassador François Bujon de l'Estang and the arrival of Jean-David Levitte, who had spent several years at the U.N. Those who at that time looked at American policy mainly from the angle of the U.N. could not fully realize the extent to which Colin Powell, the champion of a resort to the U.N. in order to legitimize the move against Iraq, was merely a secondary actor in George Bush's play, even if he was a fine tactician.

Tradition and habits suggested that American foreign policy is made by the State Department. This is a mistake. Kissinger had been the main foreign policymaker when he was national security adviser. Now, one didn't understand well enough that a horde of neoconservatives with radical and bizarre ideas had to be taken seriously. As they themselves explained it (especially the former Republican leader of the House of Representatives Newt Gingrich), the State Department has a mania for conciliation, small steps and small designs, and a predominant concern for the opinion of others, whereas for the neoconservatives force is the privileged expression of power, and international institutions were just so many traps for the U.S.

Bozo: Wasn't there also a sort of boomerang effect of traditional French policy which consists, since the Cuban crisis of 1962, of expressing unshakeable solidarity in case of a major threat, while reserving for France the right to dissent on everything else? By not acting in Iraq as one had in Cuba, wasn't France exposing itself to the charge of betraying America?

Hoffmann: Are allies obliged to obey as automatons when they see a catastrophe coming? Independently of this, the attitude that had been bluntly defined by George Bush after September 11: "You are either for us or against us," didn't leave any real margin for maneuver. In the past, France had opposed the United States in the vote of 1954 about the European Defense Community, on Vietnam, NATO, on the dollar; either French "dissidence" was rather theoretical, or it did not threaten an interest deemed vital by Washington, or else the Americans had a pressing interest in finding an accommodation. In 2002–2003, Bush's team decided that Iraq constituted a "vital" threat to the nation, that no compromise was desirable and that any dissidence would be punished. This is what is fundamentally new.

Bozo: Can't one say that the crisis is the result of an excessive French confidence in the Franco-American relation?

Hoffmann: You are right. And also, an excessive confidence in the permanence of a certain form of American leadership which, until Bush the Second, had tried to take allies into account, an attitude shaped by the Cold War and the desire to distinguish the conduct of the United States from the hegemonic kind of behavior manifested by the Soviet Union. One must remember the extent to which, just two years ago, the French Foreign Minister Hubert Védrine could maintain confident, strong relations with Madeleine Albright despite all their divergences, and she has written about this. The sort of men and women who defined foreign policy around Bill Clinton, and Clinton himself, were, as de Gaulle had said of John F. Kennedy, "Europeans" with whom one could discuss and with whom one could disagree, but who, despite the difference in power, were actually partners. The French government did not understand soon enough the extent to which the new American team was sure of itself and dominating. When all the sources are available, it will be interesting to see how the French and probably the British too have been taken by surprise and realized too late that the Americans had decided to wage this war under any circumstances. If one analyzes a succession of facts only from the point of view of classical diplomatic history, one would understand how far things progressed methodically, step-by-step, in this direction. Ultimately, everything was brought back to terrorism. It is surprising to see how many people close to the United States let themselves be lulled because they spoke to Colin Powell and to the State Department and because Bush shrewdly knew how to give the impression that he did not know what his ultimate decision would be. Europeans put too much trust in their interlocutor: "if they had really been determined not to listen to us under any circumstances, they would have told us," they naïvely thought. The Americans were quite cunning; it was only in January 2002 that they announced to their allies that everything was decided and that what was happening at the U.N. was only designed to appease Tony Blair, who wanted a validation of the war by the U.N.

Unfortunately, the "wise men," those moderate and judicious Americans who led American diplomacy after 1945 belonged to a bygone age. The French did not understand to what extent the teams of the two Presidents Bush were totally different from one another, or the extent to which a large part of the current situation was inspired by an utter contempt for the father's team. This was indeed rather difficult to perceive at first, not only because of the role played by the Secretary of State of the first Bush, James Baker, in order to get the second one elected, even though it seems he had serious reservations on the second Bush's later policies. Nor do I think that the French have sufficiently understood the importance of domestic factors. If there is one country in which one cannot understand foreign policy without linking it to domestic politics, it is the United States. But most French still perceive things in a much too classical manner. They did not realize that the Bush administration was determined to discredit France, to make people believe that France would under no circumstances ever support the Americans and British against Saddam, whereas one knew quite well in Washington since December 2002 how many soldiers France was willing to send if there was an agreement on a joint military operation.

Bozo: This brings us back to the problem of French responsibility. Don't you think that the French position, which was quite balanced in the fall of 2002, halfway between Gerhard Schroeder's pacifism and Tony Blair's endorsement of the American position, was brutally abandoned at the time of the fortieth anniversary of the Franco-German treaty, in January 2003, and changed into a kind of endorsement of the German position? Wasn't France running the risk of being accused of inconstancy or opportunism?

Hoffmann: I think that this apparent change can be explained by the fact that the French had just discovered, through information given to the French permanent representative at the

U.N., Jean-Marc de la Sablière, by his American colleague John Negroponte, that war had been decided upon (now we know that it had been decided much earlier, in the summer of 2002 and indeed prepared since the fall of 2001), and that consequently for the United States the U.N. phase was over, that the Resolution 1441, this compromise that had been painfully negotiated in October-November 2002 by Colin Powell and Dominique de Villepin, had given the U.S. everything it had needed to justify an intervention in Iraq, and that the second resolution which was being so intensely discussed was just a maneuver aimed at, first satisfying Blair and, secondly, obliging the members of the Security Council to make an explicit choice. The French were furious to see to what extent the Americans had fooled them.

Bozo: I share your explanation of the change in the French position in January, but wasn't there a typically "Chiracian" if not "Gaullian" side to this sudden change of tack?

Hoffmann: Maybe. But I don't think that, even if the French position had taken a more diplomatic and less "Gaullian" turn, it would have changed anything. France wanted to pursue the inspections before any resort to force; the United States wanted to put an end to those inspections and start military operations.

Bozo: But hasn't the French attitude mainly helped the hawks? It has been said that de Villepin had "lost Powell" at the end of January in mentioning then a possible French veto at the time of a Security Council meeting whose agenda was terrorism, which Powell had considered a bad trick. Even if Powell had indeed rejoined the "war camp" at the end of 2002, this episode has been used to deprive the French position of credibility.

Hoffmann: Indeed, Colin Powell had been "turned" for a long time. He may have been shocked by the firmness of de Villepin's statements in New York on that day, but one must say that Powell, who is an attractive person, is however not lacking a certain vanity, and he was in a tough position. This being said, why is it shocking that Dominique de Villepin should talk about Iraq during a meeting on terrorism? It was the Americans who amalgamated the two subjects. In any case, bad faith was not lacking on Powell's side either. Thus, in March 2003, he interpreted Chirac's statement that "in no circumstance" would France vote for the second resolution, to mean that the French president had said that in no circumstance would he approve any resort to force; the media endorsed this without even looking at the actual text of Chirac's statement. Where responsibilities mainly lie there is not very much in doubt.

Bozo: Aren't you, perhaps because of your own situation, overly indulgent toward French policy? Many in France have judged this shift of the French position at the end of January 2001 as too brutal, and as to the policy followed later as counterproductive. Wouldn't Mitterrand have been much more subtle, as in the previous crisis with Iraq in 1990?

Hoffmann: We can discuss tactics, to be sure, but on substance I agreed with the French policy. It might have been better presented and formulated, but I think that in any case even if Chirac had been more low-key in his statements, and if French diplomacy had asserted more firmly that it shared America's will to force Iraq to meet its commitments toward the U.N., I am not sure that things would have been different; the result would have been the same. I am not sure that things would have been better under Mitterrand. He would have played the role of the Sphinx. The Gaullian tendency to lead with the chin, as the Americans often say, entails dangers, to be sure. But Mitterrand sometimes gave the impression that his "yes" was perhaps "no" and vice versa, which is not necessarily a good thing. I don't see him endorsing regime change in Baghdad.

Bozo: Let us get to the problem of the veto. Once one saw that war would occur, because the Americans had decided it, wasn't it better to accept this, knowing that preventing the U.S. from obtaining a U.N. endorsement would not stop them, wasn't it preferable to avoid useless confrontation and thereby to play into the hands of the hawks, since it confirmed the impotence if not the nefarious character of the U.N., while justifying the hawks' distrust of France?

Hoffmann: I have the impression that what the French leaders had hoped for was that the Americans would accept a tacit compromise, which France proposed, and which consisted in saying "Abstain from presenting a second resolution, first because you will not have the necessary votes in the Security Council and, secondly, because Resolution 1441 is ambiguous enough to be presented by you as allowing a resort to force. We would agree to disagree. This would avoid a vote which would oblige us either to oppose you or to endorse you." The Americans, it seems, rejected this offer, partly because they believed that they *would* have the nine votes they needed and partly because they had to give satisfaction to Blair, who wanted to keep this second resolution alive in order to persuade his public opinion. The result was, from the American viewpoint, a bad maneuver since they did *not* have the nine votes. In any case, they were no longer in any mood to accept compromise proposals and they saw absolutely nothing wrong in presenting France as the Judas of that story.

Bozo: Still, on the French side, one finds well-known features of French foreign policy and diplomatic culture. France's game confirmed what many believe, that this culture shows at times an excessive taste for rhetoric, even incantation. Is the Security Council just a stage?

Hoffmann: This is true, but the Security Council is *also* a stage and from the moment George Bush said, "I absolutely want a vote so that people can be counted," he pushed the French into their ultimate position.

Bozo: There is a paradox on the French side: in order to prevent the Americans from obtaining a majority in the Security Council, which made it unnecessary for France to use a veto, France had to threaten the use of a veto but the impression of being an obstructionist was thereby created even if the veto wasn't used.

Hoffmann: Yes. What exasperated Washington was Dominique de Villepin going to talk to various countries in Africa, and thus contributing to deprive Bush and Blair of the majority that they had expected. If there had been nine or ten votes supporting the United States, the impression in public opinion would have been that the majority of the Security Council members supported the U.S., whether the French vetoed the resolution or not; hence the anger in Washington and London.

Bozo: Didn't French diplomacy thus take the risk of feeding the most hostile criticism, in particular the charge of having led a real anti-American campaign? And even though there had been, at the end, no veto, hasn't France greatly mortgaged the future of French-American relations for a rather debatable advantage: the failure of the second resolution?

Hoffmann: Maybe, but in order to avoid such a Franco-American crisis, did one have to make possible the legitimation by the

Security Council of a war based on highly debatable calculations and assumptions? Was a prolongation of the U.N. inspections, with a specific mandate from the U.N. to those inspectors, in itself an anti-American idea? In any case, the argument that de Villepin made is not without importance: it was necessary that one Western country endowed with the right of veto try to treat the Muslim world with respect in order to prevent a "clash of civilizations." This is not an absurd position.

2

A NEW AMERICAN IMPERIALISM

Rupture or Continuity?

Bozo: Let us try to place the present phase in time by asking the classical historian's question: is this a break with the past or is there continuity? There is an excessive tendency to emphasize the novelty of this phase even though, in a number of aspects, it can be seen as part of a permanent tendency. You have written about the specificity of recent events, the latest episode of this long story, but you have shown that there is a constant oscillation between the temptation of the crusade and that of withdrawal; this is, you argue, the manifestation of an exceptionalism that is indeed at the heart of American foreign policy. Isn't this new development the latest form of the crusade?

Hoffmann: For more than a century after its independence, America's privileged geographic situation was the main component of foreign policy: far enough from Europe and Asia to be safe and to be able to protect itself from involvement in any other nation's affairs; capable, at the same time, of extending its borders without any real opposition. A second component has been the American institutional system; it is the greatest representative of democracy, the role of the legislature and of civil society in foreign affairs is larger than anywhere else. Hence America's rejection of the rule of force, which characterized European diplomacy, and its rejection of a certain aristocratic conception of that diplomacy; these features defined the particular mission of America. At the same time, this grand missionary definition left room for contradictions. First, historically the pretensions to universality were perfectly compatible with a defense of the national interest as fierce as that of other countries: the brutal behavior involved in American territorial expansion during the nineteenth and early twentieth centuries bear witness to this. Secondly, the fundamental contradictions came from the two very different forms that American exceptionalism has had, what I have called the Wilsonian syndrome. The first form, less relevant once the U.S. grew in power, is isolationism, which resulted from the legacy of the Founding Fathers: not letting oneself be entangled in alliances. This is what led Wilson to declare, when the First World War broke out, that the United States was too proud to fight because Americans considered themselves as a beacon for mankind and thus did not have to get involved in other nations' battles. The other form is more militant, aimed at guaranteeing a world made safe for democracy by building international institutions, good both for the promotion of American interests and for the accomplishment of its mission, even if these institutions had to be organized so as to minimize the risk of involvement through alliances, about which the U.S. remained as distrustful as ever. Those two forms of exceptionalism showed the same desire to protect and, in the second case, even to project those American values and institutions which made the U.S. unique in the eyes of Americans. Thirdly, let me add that the militant form of exceptionalism itself has two different faces: that of the sheriff always ready to resort to force in order to crush the bad guys, to protect the little ones, and to insure the triumph of goodness—Wilson himself didn't hesitate to use a big stick in Latin America—and the face of the missionary who wants to emancipate and to "lift" other nations. When the United States refused to join the League of Nations after the First World War, it was clear that Wilson had failed to overcome these contradictions.

On the contrary, the containment strategy after 1947 allowed the U.S. in the context of the cold war to achieve a remarkable synthesis between power politics and American exceptionalism. The U.S. of course sought superiority, especially military, but at the service of a just cause, the fight against Communism, in the framework of international democratic institutions. It is perfectly possible to interpret the present phase through the prism of what I have just described. There has been a kind of rediscovery of the usefulness of power as a necessary ingredient for both of the militant faces of American exceptionalism. However, this underestimates the extent to which the present phase is a departure from the past; what is new today is that exceptionalism is almost exclusively based on military power. Alterations could already be read between the lines of the *Defense Planning Guide* of 1992, nicknamed "the masterpiece of Dick Cheney." It introduced explicitly the possible necessity of unilateral action, it stressed the preventive use of force, and highlighted the usefulness of a nuclear arsenal powerful enough to deter the development of nuclear programs in other countries. The point was clearly to impose constraints on the allies of the United States, while proposing a strategy of deterring all rivals and of allowing interventions anywhere. Although at the time this didn't lead to a rupture, one could already feel the tension between a will to liberate American forces from constraints and the existence of alliances and agreements that had been working for forty years or more. Today, it is no longer the assertion of a doctrine of national interest pure and simple, it is something profoundly new which takes us very far away from the Wilsonian syndrome. Instead of expressing ideals or proposing a mission, instead of calling on the U.S. to cultivate its own garden or, inversely, to build with other countries a multilateral system at the service of common objectives, exceptionalism from now on means only seeing oneself as the only superpower and acting as such. In other words, exceptionalism (in fact if not in rhetoric) is reduced only to the question of means.

Bozo: Let us get back to the cold war, a decisive period, obviously, for American life. To be sure it is a war that is over; one can even ask if September 11 was the true final moment. But one can ask also if we don't find today, mutatis mutandis, a kind of prolongation. Some members of the Bush administration have not hesitated to compare the year 2001 to the year 1947 when the strategy of containment was adopted, the idea being that today, as in 1947, one was entering a new era which required an equally new grand strategy: containment then, war against terrorism today. Is this war becoming a paradigm of the international system, just like the cold war earlier? Are we indeed in a new and lasting era?

Hoffmann: There are possible parallels. The founders of the new strategy of containment all had a very sharp perception of the new might of the U.S. The rest of the west and Asia were in very bad shape, and the only rival, the Soviet Union of Stalin, could be confronted only by a choice between two options. One was preventive action, at least as long as the U.S. had the monopoly of nuclear weapons, i.e., until 1949. As for containment, it became the official doctrine and led to military alliances with the countries that had to be preserved from Soviet domination. This realism of might, as I have said, was tempered by various calls to idealism that Wilson in his day would have approved. The fight against communism was not presented simply as a test of force but as a crusade of good against evil. The creation of an important network of international and regional organizations was part of the test of strength, but it was also considered as a policy at the service of peace and welfare. There was, in other words, a synthesis, a successful one, of the two traditional components of exceptionalism even if the balance sheet of forty years of containment is mixed. What was good about it, in addition to the absence of any major East-West confrontation, was the rebirth of Western Europe and Japan as the protégés of Washington, the skillful management of the break between China and the Soviet Union, the acrobatic success of turning into clients both Israel and many Arab countries, etc. But let us not forget the downside, beginning with Vietnam, a bitter demonstration of the limits of doctrines and of the impotence of force in certain situations, and also a demonstration of the limits of America's attractiveness in the rest of the world and of America's internal fragility—many points which present-day political leaders have neglected.

The parallel has its limits. It is easier and more convincing to assert that the confrontation of the two superpowers was really the dominant problem after 1945 than to state today that the fight against terrorism has the same importance. As Hubert Védrine has said very rightly, there are many other major problems, in the present world: the proliferation of weapons of mass destruction, failed states leading to conflicts, the effects of globalization, etc., and none of those can be resolved by the United States alone. In addition, despite the militarization of the cold war, the Americans had not forgotten the economic dimension, hence the Marshall Plan, or cultural policy. Today everything seems subordinated to the use of force. Now, the war against terrorism requires not only police or military action but a complex treatment of its many causes, a long-term task which requires self-criticism in the whole of the Western world. During the cold war, the Americans had understood that in order to oppose Soviet military power, they had to be surrounded by allies and engaged in international institutions. Even Zbigniew Brzezinski, not a man whom one can accuse of modesty when the task was the use of American might, understood this very well. Look at his book, *Political Power: USA/USSR* (by Zbigniew Brzezinski and Samuel P. Huntington; Harmondsworth; New York: Penguin Books, 1977, c1964); this book has been, in my opinion, undervalued. It compares the way in which the Soviets and the Americans dealt with their allies; the two authors showed how the United States, in order to distinguish itself from the Soviets, had given to the allies an importance which, objectively, from the point of view of hard power only, was debatable. It allowed those allies, except of course in Latin America, to challenge their protector at times (remember Suez, the European Defense Community, Willy Brandt's détente policy, the entry of Eurocommunists into the Italian Left). Things have changed. The imperial republic that Aron wrote about in the 1970s seems very pale compared to the present one.

Bozo: It is nevertheless interesting to stop more precisely at the end of the cold war in the eighties, for two reasons. First, didn't the neoconservatives who influence American foreign policy today, like Richard Perle and Paul Wolfowitz, manifest themselves first under Reagan? Also the idea of an American victory in the cold war, which, according to many conservative views, was obtained thanks to Reagan's policy of might, has led to a certain triumphalism which explains, perhaps, present tendencies. After all, if the U.S. has prevailed over the Soviet Union, it can prevail over any other challenge. In this sense, isn't Bush Junior more Reaganesque than his father, even though the latter was the vice president and successor to Reagan?

Hoffmann: There is indeed in a sense a Reaganesque origin to the present policy. But this idea has to be considerably modified. Reagan was less coherent or obstinate than is generally believed. To be sure, in the beginning, he presented himself as the sheriff; he denounced the "evil empire," he deployed missiles in Europe, he dreamed of star wars, etc. But despite everything that was a little simplistic about him, he never treated allies the way the current administration does. Especially after 1984—and no Democrat would have predicted it—he reopened nuclear arms limitation talks and then helped Gorbachev, without ever trying to push the Russians to the limit. The Reagan of the final years relied on his Secretary of State, George Shultz, who thought that one had to cooperate with the Europeans even when it wasn't easy, and who encouraged Reagan in the idea that one should not exploit the weakness of the Soviet Union, an idea which was, after all, quite remarkable, and which the first President Bush adopted later. And then there had been the famous summit meeting in Reykjavik, October 11–12, 1986, where, face to face with Gorbachev, Reagan practically posed as the champion of universal nuclear disarmament, thus horrifying people like Richard Perle. For all those reasons, the idea of a pure and simple American victory in the cold war is debatable and the neoconservatives know it well. For them, Reagan and after him, Bush the First, had not really sufficiently taken advantage at that time of the Soviet Union's bankruptcy. This doesn't prevent them from entertaining the legend, which goes, indeed, in that direction.

In short, as many of the ideas of the Reagan of 1981–1983 had been propagated by people who were neophytes at the time, and whom one finds again, like Perle, in the current administration, these same men had later been disappointed by Reagan and they were even more disappointed by Bush the First, both having been guilty of "weakness" toward the Soviet Union, and Bush the First being accused in addition of failing to overthrow Saddam Hussein after the victory in the Gulf War by not sending American forces to Baghdad. This explains where they have seen in the coming to power of Bush the son, especially after September 11, an opportunity to catch up with lost time. Finally, as a last remark on Reagan, one understands today when one looks at the drafts of his speeches, that he gave primary importance to the word; execution did not worry him much. Now, I think that the neoconservatives have drawn from the Reagan experience the conclusion that one should not leave to the president the responsibility of carrying out a policy and that it was they who should do so. Unfortunately they have recently found the occasion to put this precept into practice.

Bozo: Let us turn to the immediate post-cold-war period and the policy of Bush the father, if only in order to show that the contrast can hardly be greater as that between him and his own son. Unilateralism prevails today; the policy of the first Bush was characterized by multilateralism. After the first Gulf War, hadn't he announced the coming of a "new world order" of which the foundation would have been the United Nations? Why did America, now that it was the only superpower, return then to the letter of the U.N. Charter, and why was this moment so brief?

Hoffmann: Unlike the war of 2003, the war against Iraq in 1991—the first conflict after the cold war—had been led by the United States under the aegis of the United Nations. In many ways, it meant the consecration of the attempt at resurrecting the collective security system of the U.N. which the Americans had established in 1945. It is in fact not surprising that after the Gulf War, the administration of Bush the First had wanted to turn this episode into a sort of second foundation of the U.N. Indeed, it was that same logic which had allowed the Bush administration at the end of hostilities to reject any idea of "going to Baghdad." The advisors to Bush the First believed that the supreme mistake of the United States would have been to intervene in the internal affairs of Iraq. Brent Scowcroft, the National Security Advisor, said, "Saddam Hussein has committed horrible crimes but it is not our role to intervene; we wouldn't know who is the good guy and who is the bad one in that country." As for Colin Powell, head of the armed forces at the time, he said that he could not imagine a more stupid policy than that of sending the American army to Baghdad. Above all, the anti-Saddam coalition would have exploded if the Americans had gone beyond the liberation of Kuwait, and the White House didn't want to take such a risk. I think this is how the first Bush definitively lost any support among the neoconservatives. But he was logical; he thought, and so did his advisors, that a new world order would be possible with the United Nations as the framework, and he did not want to take the risk of having this policy fail by launching the adventure of invading Iraq.

Why this resolutely multilateral policy didn't last longer can easily be understood with the benefit of hindsight. The idea of a new world order was simply too far away from international reality. The end of the Soviet empire did not unveil a quiet world landscape, and ethnic conflicts, often horribly bloody as in the Balkans, raised very difficult questions. Should one intervene, and if the answer is yes, where and on whose side? These questions provoked a debate between the idealists who supported the *droit d'ingérence*, i.e., the right to intervene, and the realists who rejected the idea that foreign policy could be reduced to "social work." Moreover, in those circumstances, the allies began to disagree among themselves, as one saw as early as 1991, over the drama of Yugoslavia. If one adds to this the desire of public opinion to concentrate on domestic matters—Bill Clinton understood this in 1992—and the determination of the military to avoid a new Vietnam, one understands why this multilateral moment did not last.

Bozo: Let's talk of Clinton. Of course, one cannot find two more different presidents than Clinton and his successor. At the same time, there are two similarities despite their evident differences in character and ideological profile. First, both come to power with a will to disengage: Clinton, as you have said, by giving priority to economic and social issues, and Bush Junior by advocating a concentration of foreign policy on purely national interests, which entailed a kind of international "humility" and a degree of retreat. One forgets that this was the priority he and Ms. Rice announced before September 11, but both Bush and Clinton were quickly caught up by international imperatives and the need for American leadership. Secondly, one can ask if there isn't, in effect, a certain continuity between the two presidencies. Wasn't there already under Clinton a certain unilateralist temptation which expressed itself in frequent impatience toward allies, a certain distrust of the achievements of multilateralism, such as arms control, and a tendency to proclaim, as Madeleine Albright did, that the United States was the "indispensable" nation?

Hoffmann: It is true that for Clinton the essential was the economy. When he arrived in the White House in January 1993, he didn't really have any philosophy in foreign policy and he was almost proud of that; moreover, the era of "doctrines" seemed to be over. The doctrine which his national security advisor, Tony Lake, tried to define, was the propagation of democracy in the world. That was it. It's great, but it didn't give you a strategy in foreign policy matters and, moreover, it didn't last very long and the Clinton administration found itself swept from one crisis to another. Indeed, there was a great deal of muddling; for instance, after the fiasco of the intervention of Somalia, nothing was done by the United States, or by the U.N., in order to prevent or stop the genocide in Rwanda. In the Balkans, it is true that the Americans, after having first left the leadership position to the Europeans, finally intervened decisively in Bosnia and in Kosovo. But if it was ultimately caught up by the necessity of leadership, the Clinton administration on the whole was far from giving the impression of a limitless will to power. Bill Clinton himself was the least arrogant or the least hierarchical of leaders. During this time, the hard-line Republican right organized and gradually took control of Congress and of the media and prepared its coming to power with the involuntary help of Clinton: the Republican Right exploited with virtuosity the Lewinsky affair so that at the end of his mandate Clinton could not get anything adopted by Congress, hence his decision not to submit to the Senate various controversial treaties, so when Bush the son, about whom nobody knew anything, arrived, the ground was prepared.

Concerning Madeleine Albright, one has to recognize that, despite her bombastic statements, she was of European origin and saw herself as a kind of hyphen between Europe and the United States. Her boasts were those of a European immigrant grateful to America for having helped the liberation of Eastern Europe. If one had told her at the time that one would end up with a kind of triumphant contempt for international law and organizations, she would have been highly indignant. She was annoyed frequently by European resistance on this or that issue, notably about the enlargement of NATO, but her irritation never took the form of threatening language, which seems fundamentally new to me. What she said was limited to, "We see farther than you do," but she did not say, "If you do not follow us you will have to pay for it," so of course she celebrated the "indispensable" nation but she did not devalue others, which is the unprecedented reality in 2003. If the Americans see farther, are more lucid, and know from the start what the general interest is, why pay attention to others?

Coming to George W. Bush, it is true that during his election campaign he talked about a necessary "humility" in foreign policy. He repeated that the United States did not have any vocation to indulge in nation-building, a term he used with a tone of contempt and sarcasm. The American army is not made to escort children to school, Ms. Rice had said in an immortal formula, à propos of Kosovo. However, when he was elected, while Bush knew what he would *not* do, he had no clear idea about what he *would* do. In international economic policy, should one persist in a strategy of opening borders, of free trade, or would one take a series of protectionist measures? In political matters, the doctrine which seemed to be popular in early 2001 was the return to realism: concentrate on those conflicts which would have an effect on the global balance of power, or on a major regional balance, and withdraw from conflicts which did not have such importance, like those that were tearing up Africa, or those which were hopeless, such as the Palestinian question. However, it was not realism that prevailed, even a few months before the different policy which came to the fore after September 11.

Bozo: To conclude, you have no doubt that the present American foreign policy *is* a break with the past?

Hoffmann: The break is much more important than continuity. After the United States became the only superpower, there was at first, under Bush the father and Clinton, a continuation of "directed multilateralism" until 2001. After that, one switches to triumphant unilateralism. After September 11 there was a universal declaration of war on terrorism and the legitimation of the new exceptionalism, expressed in the *National Security Strategy of the United States* of September 2002, a kind of smorgasbord which mentions both American primacy and traditional balance of power while resorting to traditional rhetoric ("we will work actively to bring the hope of democracy, of development, of markets and of free trade to every corner of the earth"). This text talks both of organizing coalitions but also of not being afraid of acting alone in order to protect oneself. It contains all the new aspects of exceptionalism: the doctrine of preventive action, the stress on threats represented by rogue states which try to acquire weapons of mass destruction, "reject fundamental human values and hate the United States for what it represents," the promise to preserve the necessary capacity to prevent any attempt by any state to impose its will on the United States and its allies and to deter adversaries from building up forces which would be equal or superior to America's and, last but not least, the will to protect American citizens against the international criminal court. All of this was made possible by September 11. The president found in those criminal acts not only the rationale that the administration had lacked at home and abroad, but a lever usable in order to increase his own and America's might, and his and his partisans' grip on the nation.

3

SEPTEMBER 11

Divine Surprise?

Bozo: Let us now address the sequence of events which, after the attack of September 11, led to the Iraqi crisis. One can now see that it was a crisis foretold. Therefore one can ask whether the effect of September 11 has, if not transformed America, at least weighed on its choices in a way that one had not imagined at the time, and which explains the Iraqi adventure. Or else should one talk of a "divine surprise," an event which was instrumentalized by some so that they could impose their program? These two interpretations are actually not mutually exclusive. The question deserves that we look more closely at certain points and at the decisive event. I have the impression that you were immediately skeptical about the

When France fell, in June 1940, and the old monarchist Marshall Pétain came to power, Charles Maurras, the old reactionary leader of the far right, wrote that the defeat of France, having made Pétain's coming to power possible, was a "divine surprise."

revolutionary significance of September 11 and this is how I interpret an article you published in *The American Prospect* on November 19, 2001, called, "Why Don't They Like Us?" Three years later, do you still stick to this analysis which, deep down, minimizes the degree to which this event was a historical break?

Hoffmann: I don't think I minimized the characteristics and implications of the event itself, but what I wanted to say was that first of all we had to understand it. What I did underestimate at the time was the fact that, for many of the people around Donald Rumsfeld and Dick Cheney, this was the long-awaited opportunity not simply to wage a fight against terrorism, but also to get their revenge against Iraq, even if it was not immediately obvious that American public opinion would be persuaded to amalgamate bin Laden and Saddam Hussein. In this respect, one can indeed talk of a "divine surprise." To stick to September 11, I think that the Bush administration had if not exaggerated its significance, at least wanted quite deliberately to give it a global, undifferentiated meaning. If terrorism means the deliberate attack against innocent people, shouldn't we distinguish different situations? Did one need to equate the many reasons for resorting to terror: the will to self-determination, as in the case of the Palestinians and the Chechens; the struggle for a territory, as in Kashmir; revolt against a repressive state (in the Sudan or in Latin America or in the Algeria of the 1990s), or a holy war, as in the case of al Qaeda, etc., etc.? A single definition cannot fit all, and limiting oneself to the character of the acts without examining the motivations is a mistake. To this add the problem of choosing the best way of fighting terror. Should one use the police and the judiciary, or should one resort to military actions indifferent to the sovereignty of states and to international law, which proscribes the preventive resort to force? Should one call on a coalition of states or is it above all an American war? Should one go after all the terrorist groups in the world, or concentrate on the threats to American lives and liberty? Behind all those questions, I felt there was a risk of indefinite extension of the war against terrorism. This is indeed what happened. Since September 11, the Bush administration has extended its fight against transnational terrorist groups by going after states which allegedly sheltered such groups. But doesn't the al Qaeda network find shelter in very many countries, including the United States? Bush has also denounced states which possess weapons of mass destruction, while excluding from that list of states Israel, India, and Pakistan. All of this undermines world order and incites some countries to divert the American doctrine to their own purposes: the Indians against the Pakistanis, the Russians against the Chechens, the Sharon government against not only Palestinian terrorists, but also against the Palestinian authority and Arafat. Thus, distinctions have been blurred that a more lucid America should have been capable of preserving. In fact the rhetoric of the "axis of evil" has justified a genuine imperial overstretch.

Before the traumatism of September 11, the tendency, discussed in the previous chapter on the new American exceptionalism, was a doctrine seeking a cause. After September 11 a cause was found: the war against world terrorism, against terrorists and the states that protect them; this program had the advantage of serving as a lever in order to mobilize opinion, smother political controversies and seduce both idealists and realists. One would defend the national interest while emphasizing the indispensable role of the United States, by proclaiming that the fight against terrorism was a fight that concerned the whole world: defense of interests and moralism, might and values, sheriff and missionary all united for the same cause. Faced with this logic, which emerged immediately after September 11, I tried to insist on the fact that the phenomenon of terrorism is profoundly heterogeneous because it is the joint effect of globalization, which opens borders, of the flaws of the international system, of political, economic, and spiritual opposition to the West, as well as an indication of the decrepitude of sovereignty and a reflection of the innumerable injustices in the world. Could all those issues be squeezed into the straitjacket of antiterrorism and dealt with primarily by military means? I doubted it then and I still doubt it.

Bozo: Let us admit, as you say, that the terrorist phenomenon and its ramifications have been homogenized by the United States after September 11. A question remains: didn't this proclamation of the global and central character of the phenomenon produce a certain reality? Once again, the parallel with the early cold war period comes to mind. There had perhaps been an overestimation of the Soviet threat by the United States in 1947, but the threat was thereby confirmed, and the cold war entered into international affairs and became an undeniable reality. Isn't it the same today with the war against terrorism, which, from now on, shapes the international system?

Hoffmann: No doubt, first because declaring war on terrorism is likely to fuel the will to fight of the terrorists, happy, so to speak, to be recognized, and because this same combativeness is likely to be heightened by American policy in other domains such as the Israel-Palestinian conflict: there results a concatenation of action and reaction; moreover, once the dominant power decides that the international system is organized around one issue, that issue becomes ipso facto the main one. However, the differences between the cold war and the present case are important. The United States, despite its anticommunist rhetoric, learned to treat differently the Soviet Union, Tito's Yugoslavia and, later, a Red China that was increasingly deviant. Moreover, the problem raised by the Soviet Union was the classical one of a revolutionary state with hegemonic pretensions. Terrorism is what de Gaulle would have called an "ungraspable" (*insaisissable*) phenomenon, and to assimilate it to an interstate phenomenon, such as the proliferation of weapons of mass destruction, is a dangerous mixing of types. Yesterday's international system was really organized around the bipolar confrontation. The present-day unipolar system does not turn around the problem of terrorism, at least not yet. It is only the American analysis which could lead to such a result through unfortunate amalgamation.

Bozo: Let us now come to the impact of the event on the United States. One sees today more clearly how much the country has changed after September 11. What are the transformations?

Hoffmann: Yes, it took some time before one discovered the scope of the trauma. To be sure, during the cold war, the awareness of vulnerability was very real because of the threat of atomic war. But it remained abstract. War over Cuba or Berlin had been avoided and there existed therefore a certain sense of immunity paradoxically provided by deterrence. The worst never happened. This time, not only did it happen but the strikes came from some unknowns; they were capable of striking anyone, anywhere. It is true that December 7, 1940—the attack on Pearl Harbor—remains engraved in collective memory, but it was long ago. On September 11 the role of television was fundamental: the spectacle of the attack, repeated thousands of times, and the fact that those towers collapsed in twenty minutes, over thousands of people, these were events and images that gave nightmares to Americans, quite understandably. The effect was absolutely decisive.

However, mass terror in the public appeared only gradually over time. In this respect September 11 had much more of a political impact than the Soviet threat in 1947. And America's leaders, especially the neoconservatives, have drawn all the consequences from this: the end of containment, the doctrine of preventive war, all kinds of things which were excluded in 1948–1949, because Europe at that time was a hostage to Soviet power, despite the huge military superiority of the United States.

Bozo: But one has to recognize that in the first two months—I am thinking about the war against the Taliban in the fall of 2001—the reaction of the United States was relatively measured, adapted, and even to some extent contained, despite a rhetoric which already stressed the war against terrorism.

Hoffmann: Yes, but this didn't last long. Afghanistan provoked a general consensus at home and abroad. It is true that if Bush had not reacted in order to prove that a country which shelters terrorists will be heavily punished, he would have run the risk of being outflanked on his right by the Democrats. As his team was one which had mobilized itself against the weaknesses of others, and particularly of the previous administration, it was easy for them to fall into activism. We will never know if the Democrats would have done the same. Some former officials of the Clinton administration have told me that Gore, if he had been elected in 2000, would also have ultimately declared war against Iraq, but I think events would have been quite different. The members of the Bush administration and their supporters were above all eager to put an end to what were in their eyes the slightly soft doctrines of the cold war days. They were determined not to treat the terrorists and the states accused of being terrorist themselves as the

Soviet Union had been treated, when all is said and done, i.e., by containment and by accepting a dialogue with it.

Bozo: Let us go back to what seems to be your fundamental idea, that September 11 was for some a "divine surprise." Does not this interpretation smack a little too much of a conspiracy theory? In this vein, some have said, as was once said of Pearl Harbor, that one let September 11 happen in order to justify everything that followed, including the war in Iraq. It is disconcerting to see how such an enormity has had resonance, particularly in France.

Hoffmann: This is certainly not what I believe. However, there have been aspects which remind one of a conspiracy scenario; but these could not have developed without a genuine national trauma. I have said it: the neoconservatives had undeniably a desire for revenge. They had been outraged by the failure to liquidate Saddam Hussein at the end of the Gulf War. The lesson they drew from that episode was that one had to avoid any genuine coalition; other states should simply follow the lead of the U.S.

Bozo: Was it fatal that one would get to that point? After all, there was a debate; many influential members of the first Bush administration, such as National Security Advisor Brent Scowcroft and Secretary of State James Baker, took public positions against a unilateral American intervention in Iraq. The former president himself probably discussed the issue with his son and perhaps attempted to persuade him not to follow this road. Why haven't they had more influence? One has the impression that in the summer of 2002 nothing was really yet decided.

Hoffmann: I think that there was not yet an irreversible shifting of gears; just before the summer of 2002 Colin Powell still declared that waging war against Iraq because of the fight against terrorism would transform an itch into a cancer or something like this. For Powell, things were not quite so obvious. He was still worried about excessive imprudence, against going too far; he probably thought it would have been better to concentrate on those terrorists who were threatening the U.S., not to assimilate Hamas and al Qaeda, the Ba'ath terrorists, and the Pakistani or Saudi ones, but this phase did not last long and the logic of amalgamation or globalization prevailed. It is true, as you suggested, that there was some similarity with the early period of the cold war. In 1947, one had not understood, or wanted to understand, that Moscow and the Greek Communists were not the same thing and, in 1961 Secretary of State Dean Rusk still considered China to be a satellite of Moscow. Precise comparisons between that period and this one would be interesting. Then, as today, there was a tendency not to make necessary distinctions. In other words, this propensity to generalize is not new but, I would say it again, cold-war America learned to distinguish among cases and the present-day consequences of the opposite tendency are execrable: any state in which terrorists strike can count on American support in order to legitimize its own attempt to suppress terrorism, even if its own acts have nurtured terrorism and if its methods are similar to those of the terrorists. Any country suspected of wanting to give itself chemical, nuclear, or biological weapons can be considered a rogue state, because it "might" allow terrorists to use them.

Bozo: We now come to the neoconservatives, who are so important in this case. On Iraq, they won, and imposed their program. How? Who are they? What is your analysis of this classical case of a small group that succeeds in imposing its policy?

Hoffmann: The neoconservatives knew each other for a long time. Some had been in power, others not. They followed courses in the same universities, especially the University of Chicago, where they had as a teacher the venerable Leo Strauss, who certainly did not teach them neoconservatism, but the art of reading between the lines of the texts of ancient political philosophy, and also the strategic thinker Albert Wohlstetter, who was both a tough anti-Soviet thinker and a believer in the need to stabilize the crisis between the two superpowers. Later, they were in the same institutions and research centers. As is often the case in politics, they found each other because they had common enemies. One has to recognize that, for some, the main enemies were those of Israel, even though this is a rather taboo topic in the United States. It is because of this that journals which were once liberal in the American sense, like *Commentary* or *The New Republic*, moved to the right after 1967. For others, the enemy was obviously the Soviet Union. For them, the decisive turn came in the 1970s, when they followed Senator Henry Jackson, a "tough" Democrat who was anti-Soviet and sharply critical of Nixon's and Kissinger's détente. Many met in the Committee on the Present Danger, whose purpose was to mobilize public opinion against the Soviet Union, deemed ever more mighty and threatening (we should remember that in the 1970s Raymond Aron himself began to share this quite mistaken analysis). In this committee, one found eminent hawks from both parties who, later on, ardently supported Reagan and deemed it inconceivable that a country as mighty as the United States should limit itself to a purely defensive strategy against the Soviet Union. For others, and more recently, it was above all a deep distaste for international organizations, for international law, for anything that could limit American might. Among these were theoreticians for whom it was unacceptable that the greatest power in history, a power which, in addition, was moved only by the desire to do good for all mankind, should be stopped by mosquitoes. Finally, some were obsessed by specific political issues such as Iraq or the flaws of the Arab world, which one absolutely had to transform in its entirety.

At the same time, these many kinds of neoconservatives shared a certain contempt for the clichés of "liberals" in foreign policy, particularly the idea that one had to take into account public opinion, that one should not go too far, and that the American people are deeply interested in foreign policy only when threatened. These people are fascinated by historical examples of might: the Roman Empire, eighteenth- or nineteenth-century Great Britain, an admiration that is rather rare in American history. There had of course been Theodore Roosevelt but in his days the United States was still largely isolationist and his imperial activism was limited to Latin America.

And then there was also a psychological factor. These individuals, who had thought that their moment had come with Reagan and were disappointed with the rather "soft" way the cold war ended, because they wanted the Soviet Union to fall very hard, were persuaded that, at the end of the Gulf War, Bush the First would follow their advice and push military operations into Baghdad in order to overthrow Saddam. So they were deeply frustrated by their own party. This is why one can talk of a "divine surprise," because the neoconservatives exploited magisterially the events of September 11. They knew that George Bush Junior, whose mandate had just begun, had no experience in foreign policy nor any very visible priorities, unlike Clinton in 1992, but that he was malleable and trying to distinguish himself from his father. As early as September 12 our neoconservatives went to see Dick Cheney, who probably had some regrets for not advocating going to Baghdad in 1991 when he was Secretary of Defense and they had no difficulty persuading him. Frustration and exasperation were fundamental, at the same time as a kind of triumphalism. Finally, our hour has come!

Bozo: Wasn't there at the same time something deeply right in the neoconservatives' idea that nothing is worse or more dangerous than the status quo, in an area like the Middle East, on an issue like the proliferation of weapons of mass destruction? In other words, wasn't the superiority of the neoconservatives, despite their label, that they were more revolutionary than the conservatives?

Hoffmann: Yes, I agree on this point. The whole problem was to know how to call into question the status quo. Does one do it alone, or with others? Does one invent scenarios worthy of Rabelais, which consist in using Iraq as a lever in order to push the whole of the Middle East into democracy, or does one listen to the opinion of those who warn that, if you proceed in this way, you are going to produce masses of terrorists? To state that there had been serious problems, and that one could charge Bill Clinton with not having really had ideas or methods for resolving them, this is legitimate. But in a region as explosive as the Middle East or the Muslim world should one prefer deep surgery to soft medicine?

Bozo: We'll come back to Europe later, but wasn't this language of the neoconservatives legitimated by the inaction, or the appearance of inaction, manifested by the Europeans, who were often their own worst enemies? Didn't the neoconservatives have a great opportunity here to repeat that the Europeans are incapable of acting, that they constantly emphasize the dangers of action, whether in the Middle East today or yesterday in the Balkans, and don't they thereby become the accomplices of the worst injustices or disorders? This kind of speech has had some resonance, and still does, because it seems to me that it is far from being entirely wrong.

Hoffmann: Yes, even though the Europeans are very useful to the Americans when the problem is that of nation-building, as in Afghanistan and perhaps now in Iraq. It's always the same scenario. One charges the Europeans with being passive, and when they take an initiative, one says to them, "Shut up!" On the one hand, one deters them from building a small army which, say the Americans, wouldn't be in any way useful, given the might of the United States, and on the other hand one looks at them as cowards or softies, people preoccupied by their health care or their holidays. In my opinion the accusations against the Europeans by the neoconservatives, and not only by them, are really dishonest. If the Europeans have any chance of being taken seriously, it is not simply by washing the dishes—dishes often broken by the Americans.

Bozo: Let us go back to the neoconservatives. What is their political base? What are their relations with the religious and fundamentalist far right? The French, I think, have too much of a tendency to equate them, which allows them to disqualify the neoconservatives by assimilating them to the religious right. Even if there are some common links or affinities, aren't these two very different worlds?

Hoffmann: Yes, the neoconservatives, many of whom are—let us not forget it—former liberals and sometimes even Trotskyites, are a small group of very identifiable people who are quite different from the representatives of the religious or fundamentalist right. The latter situate themselves far to the right, and are above all hostile to the evolution of social mores and social laws they detest. In domestic politics they have a real program which is deeply hostile to the state; in foreign policy they don't really have a program. Their real objective is to erase what was accomplished by the New Deal, and also the troubled legacy of the 1960s. I don't think that they and the neoconservatives have many affinities, given their origins and priorities. The neoconservatives are above all men of power, and they are a small number; the Christian right has large numbers to mobilize and they constitute an important and dominating wing of the Republican Party in the country and in Congress. The neoconservatives are embedded in the think tanks, in institutes such as the Heritage Foundation or the American Enterprise Institute. The Christian right has its churches, its television channels, its preachers, and its faithful. These are two very different worlds, brought together by some of their common dislikes but not all; the preservation of a certain religiosity, of traditional mores, and of the family are not the main concerns of the neoconservatives. Conversely, the Christian right is not really engaged in foreign policy, except for an unlimited enthusiasm for Israel, at least the Israel that fights Arabs mercilessly, hence the sympathy of fundamentalist Christians who consider Islam as a dangerous religion.

However, they share notions on which my Straussian colleague, the political philosopher Harvey Mansfield, Jr., has written a great deal, and which bring back memories of writers in the 1930s: virility and elitism. Mansfield declared at a recent meeting of the Faculty of Arts and Sciences at Harvard University that he approved the present foreign policy of the United States, because the U.S. was indeed at war, and that it was therefore impossible to give priority to the preservation of public liberties. He added that in such circumstances it is the majority which is threatened and it therefore has the right to restrict the liberties of the minority. This is a program for both foreign policy and domestic policy. Otherwise, what strikes me in the U.S. at present is not so much the rhetoric of black and white, which we are used to, but this kind of cult of force, which is radically new. After 1947, it was the Soviet Union that was denounced for practicing that cult. Today one finds it among some Americans, as if they had reread Carl Schmitt or the Italian theoreticians of fascism. This is quite serious.

Bozo: Beyond speeches and ideology, how much, according to you, have public liberties, the liberal and democratic rule of law, been affected by events since September 11? Don't Europeans, and especially the French, tend to exaggerate on this point? Moreover, three years after September 11, isn't there a beginning of a return to normalcy, as if the natural "antibodies" of American society were beginning to react?

Hoffmann: The rule of law in the United States has been affected much more seriously than the Americans admit and their friends abroad perceive. One has to understand that the mood of the public allows for that, especially a certain passivity, a tendency of public opinion to follow. Concerning people arrested on American soil, many people reassure themselves by saying, "After all, if one arrests them, there must be serious motives for that." For a long time, sending people to Guantanamo as "enemy combatants" without any lawyer or indictment appeared quite acceptable. The simple fact that the Congress adopted only a few weeks after September 11, in a climate of emergency, the famous Patriot Act, which reinforces security measures—a text of 360 pages that few Congressmen or women had read—is quite revealing. Americans are only beginning to realize that the antiterrorist tools that they have given themselves have seriously eroded their public freedoms. The Patriot Act authorizes, for instance, FBI agents to do secret searches in the homes of people suspected of being terrorists, to multiply wiretaps, or to look at the files of banks, universities, libraries, airline companies, etc., without warning. The control of the movements of foreigners is deemed necessary for internal security. Today, authorities have the right to demand that universities—in other words, my colleagues and myself—provide information on some of our students if they have the misfortune of coming from countries perceived as dangerous. France is not yet on the list! If one had invoked such measures only a few years ago, Americans would have said that this is Orwellian. This shows to what extent a country that is on the whole extremely legalistic can suddenly, under the spell of fear and emergency, put fundamental freedoms in brackets. This had already happened during the First World War and again during the Second World War and, to a lesser extent, because there was little legislation then, at the time of McCarthyism.

Resistance was at first very weak, even though it is beginning to strengthen. A number of members of Congress who voted for that law—in fact, it was adopted almost unanimously—are beginning to think that they should perhaps have read those 360 pages sooner. You are right to talk about antibodies, even if their effectiveness has just begun.

Until now, almost all the attempts to challenge the limitations of rights in court have failed. The courts have answered that in time of war the executive has extensive war powers. In a way, the notion of declaring a war against terrorism has been brilliant: everything can be turned into a direct threat against the American people. Today Bush is asking for a reinforcement of the Patriot Act which would substitute in some cases bureaucrats for judges, etc.

Guantanamo is a horrible situation from the viewpoint of individual rights, but it has not shocked enough people. Guantanamo is not an American territory and therefore the courts have at first considered that they have no jurisdiction over it. The military are those who, with an ominous slowness, select the prisoners, free some, get ready (rarely) to judge others. The Supreme Court, of course, has finally dealt with this case in the summer of 2004. One also has to remember the large number of highly conservative judges whom the executive has asked Congress, on the whole successfully, to appoint to the federal courts. If the Democrats resist, they are accused of being obstructionist or, when those proposed judges are women or blacks or Latinos, they are accused of favoring discrimination! So they limit their criticism to the most reactionary or the most shocking, and let the others slip by.

Bozo: Let us conclude on the effects of September 11. The last question I would like to ask is how one got from September 11 to the Iraqi crisis—in other words, why Iraq?

Hoffmann: Because it was easy. Indeed, one of the major contradictions is that Washington, on the one hand, asserted that Iraq was a threat for the whole world and, on the other hand, recognized almost in the same breath that it had been considerably weakened by its defeat in 1991, which was true; that it had a very mediocre army, which was true; that the regime was fundamentally detested, which was true; and that, consequently, military operations could only be successful, which wasn't wrong either. But when one compares that with the way in which the White House has carefully avoided, so far, touching that hedgehog which is North Korea, one remains amazed, especially since one knows that the nuclear threat from North Korea is genuinely dangerous. Of course, there was the irrefutable argument concerning the horrible nature of the Iraqi regime, and this is indeed the argument that my liberal friends who supported the war have relied on. For them, the main issue was not weapons of mass destruction but the need for an operation comparable to those which had been undertaken in Bosnia, in Kosovo, in East Timor, and so on. This is why many of them, at least for a while, provided support for Bush's war. In their eyes, regime change was more important than international order. Let me stress that I entirely share their horror toward Saddam's regime, but what happens to the world if the mighty give themselves the right to eliminate, without any mandate, regimes they do not like? This does not mean that the problem of murderous regimes is not a highly serious one; I will deal with it later. In this respect, by the way, the North Korean regime is not any more attractive than Saddam's.

Let me add that, in the launching of the war, oil was not a decisive factor, contrary to what has been written quite often. The Americans have always been able to import oil, even if the restrictions that they had imposed on Saddam Hussein reduced Iraq's production. To be sure, the "liberation" of the oil resources of Iraq was important insofar as the resources of Saudi Arabia were no longer as safe as before the spread of religious terrorism. However, I don't think that this objective was decisive, nor the goal of signing new contracts. Americans sincerely believed, with the help of neoconservatives, that insofar as this was an outlaw regime, and that Americans would be greeted as liberators, they would have no difficulty in putting in place a democratic regime and that this would spread a little like an oil slick throughout the Arab world. In other words, the expedition to Iraq was easy to sell and has been very well sold. The only thing lacking was the benediction of the Security Council but the people in power felt no need to have the American intervention legitimized by anyone.

4

CHRONICLE OF A WAR FORETOLD

Bozo: Let us get now to what one might call, as in 1990–1991, the logic of war. How did one get from the umpteenth Iraqi crisis to a new Gulf War, from the summer or fall of 2002 to the spring of 2003? Hence my first question, to which it is probably too early to reply with certainty, and to which historians will have to return when they have all the sources. When, according to you, was the war decided?

Hoffmann: At the end of the summer of 2002, Dick Cheney in one of his rare speeches stated his opposition to any return to the United Nations, asserted that the inspections would be of absolutely no use, and that the U.N. was incapable of putting an end to Saddam Hussein's misdeeds, etc. It is at this moment, it seems, that Colin Powell and his advisors reacted strongly: "Cheney talks as if the president has already decided on war; are we going to submit to this?" Powell, at that point, repeated to Bush his hope for an agreement at the U.N., which in his eyes was indispensable if one wanted to legitimize the military operation, and above all in order to satisfy Tony Blair. This was at the end of August. An informed source told me that the decision for war had probably already been made in July. Indeed, the recent book by Bob Woodward suggests that it was taken even earlier and prepared since November of 2002.[1] Under those conditions the Cheney speech probably aimed at both avoiding long detours in the U.N., where the Americans risked getting bogged down, and preparing public opinion. As for Bush's speech at the General Assembly of the U.N. on September 12, 2002, its main purpose was to present the official argument for war while satisfying those who hoped for a resolution in the Security Council. It has been said, indeed, that the president almost forgot this last point in his speech and caught himself at the very last minute. This indicates how little importance the U.N. had in his eyes.

Bozo: Are you suggesting that Colin Powell himself had already accepted the idea of the war even before the September 12 speech by the president at the U.N. General Assembly? And yet this speech has been largely perceived as a victory for the Secretary of State and, if not for those who wanted peace, at least for those who wanted multilateralism, but your analysis suggests that his concern was not so much to prevent war as to legitimize it.

Hoffmann: Yes, to legitimize it and at the same time to respect the commitments Bush had more or less made to the British. My source, whom I cannot name but who is perfectly respectable and trustworthy, had told me at that time that everything was already decided. Nevertheless, none of this became known because in 2002–2003 the Bush administration was a

1. *Plan of Attack* (New York: Simon & Shuster, 2004).

remarkably well-disciplined house and as a result the British and the French learned about the decision only very late. It is at that point, in the fall of 2002, that there began in the Security Council the negotiations that led to Resolution 1441, but also the deployment of American and British troops in the area. This allowed Washington and London to plan carefully for military operations over a period of time.

Bozo: But if things had been thus decided, isn't it extraordinary that nothing leaked? During that period the press did not, as far as I know, suggest that the decision had been made. This perfectly kept secret would be a very rare example in the U.S. Moreover, how could Colin Powell, whose reputation was one of integrity, lend himself to a sort of masquerade at the U.N.?

Hoffmann: I repeat, as the officials didn't tell them anything, the media couldn't get much out of them. In this whole episode, the lack of curiosity of the media has been astounding. In the United States, keeping this kind of a secret for six months is very unusual. Someday perhaps one will discover in the pages of the *New York Times* or in an essay by Bob Woodward a formula of this sort, "the information now at our disposal will allow us to say. . . ." If you read carefully Woodward's book, *Bush at War*, there isn't a word about it. Indeed, one has had to wait for his next book, *Plan of Attack*, published in the spring of 2004, and for an apology by the *New York Times*, published in May 2004, in order to get a mild form of a confession.

As for Powell, let us not forget that he is above all a good soldier. He was convinced that international legitimation was necessary and he must have expected that he would obtain the Security Council resolution which would provide it. For the rest, despite his reluctance for the military option, he became more and more influenced by the arguments that were being made against Saddam Hussein: his violations of U.N. resolutions since 1991, his lack of cooperation with the inspectors, and of course the question of the weapons of mass destruction.

Bozo: It's a little difficult to believe that a final decision for war was taken so early; this reduces the U.N. episode to a pure and simple trick. Like many others, I thought that the speech by the president on September 12 represented a real multilateral opening. Can't one imagine that what had already been decided in Washington—perhaps much earlier—was not so much war but a strategy that had a good chance to lead to war, especially because of the conditions that would be demanded of Saddam Hussein and because of the deployment of troops? The consequences of such a sequence of events, especially in terms of transatlantic relations, are rather different, I believe.

Hoffmann: Yes, it is not impossible that what was meant by "the decision has been made" was that one had decided to deploy American troops in the Middle East and to launch a military offensive unless Saddam yielded completely. But very few officials believed that Saddam would yield; indeed, I don't know of anyone who did. Moreover, they didn't really want him to yield, since the purpose was to get rid of him. As for the Europeans, they should have believed, while deciphering the march of events, that this was the American strategy.

To sum up, there was undoubtedly a decision at the highest levels for a military operation as early as the summer, but until September there was a disagreement on procedures and on the role of the United Nations. Powell won on that point because he was sensitive to the situation of Tony Blair. He must have thought that it was a "win-win" game: if Saddam capitulated to the conditions of the U.N., everything would be fine, but if he did not yield, one would be militarily ready through the troop deployment and politically ready thanks to the Security Council debate and resolution. Moreover—and this was an additional advantage—he would be eliminated.

Bozo: After the question of "when," let us move to the question of "who." What precedes suggests that one probably has to talk, rather than of a single decision, of a process of decisions leading to war, and Saddam by his attitude was in fact a part of this process. To limit oneself to the American administration, what was the role and influence of the various participants? Concerning the president himself, he has a contradictory image: on the one hand, that of a commander-in-chief in the hands of the neoconservatives and the hawks; on the other hand, there is an image of an Eisenhower-like president who allows a debate to develop around him before he makes up his mind.

Hoffmann: It is the president who, in the final analysis, makes the decisions, for obvious constitutional reasons. But it is difficult to penetrate his personality and therefore to be entirely clear about his attitude in this business. There is, it is true, a side of Bush that is direct and amiable, but there is also a side to him that Eisenhower did not have. Bush is more than a little devious and often vindictive. He doesn't hesitate to lie, either in domestic or in foreign policy. I would say that deep down he was determined to overthrow Saddam and that he was influenced in this direction by the neoconservatives while remaining "pragmatic" and fluctuating on the tactics to adopt in order to reach his goal.

Concerning the others, there is one personality which is important among those who were around the president. It is Vice President Cheney, whose role was probably decisive. He has his own group of advisors, including his own National Security Advisor, among whom the neoconservatives are very powerful. As for Donald Rumsfeld, of whom the least one can say is that he is not devious, he is even more unilateralist than Cheney; it is he, who when NATO invoked for the first time Article 5 of the North Atlantic Treaty, in order to offer its services in Afghanistan just after September 11, let it be known that he didn't need NATO! Finally there was this whole Pentagon civilian team: Wolfowitz and company, whom we have mentioned. They must have convinced the president, and Cheney's speech in August must have expressed an opinion prevalent in the White House: one had to avoid getting bogged down in a United Nations quagmire. What Powell consequently obtained was a simple detour through the U.N. for a limited period, as events demonstrated.

Bozo: Let us get back to the speech of September 12. At the time there was a kind of diplomatic-media competition between Paris and London to decide which of the two countries had played the decisive role in persuading Washington to "return" to the U.N. In your opinion was it Tony Blair, or was it Jacques Chirac—who had given an interview to the *New York Times* in which he did *not* rule out the resort to force and proposed his idea of two resolutions—who made the difference? Both? Neither?

Hoffmann: I don't think that anybody really paid attention to the interview of Jacques Chirac. I do not remember anyone on whom it had any effect. For the Americans, France was a kind of thorn in the foot because of its threat of a veto, and the purpose of Resolution 1441 was to remove that thorn. Indeed, many in Washington were persuaded that the French would end up joining the allies in order not to be isolated.

England was from the start undeniably the privileged partner. The links with Tony Blair were very much greater than with the French. From the beginning, Blair had been more eloquent and convincing than Bush in his denunciation of

Iraq's regime. The Americans knew what problems he had within his party and with public opinion and wanted to help him. However, helping him was above all a tactical preoccupation; the Americans knew that they could count on him as a strong ally, and they therefore had to give him some satisfaction, they couldn't alienate him by proving even more arrogant than they generally were. Certainly, in the outside world, one had the impression that only Blair had gotten Bush to change direction and resort to the U.N., even if things were perhaps a little more complicated.

Bozo: Under those conditions, how can one interpret Resolution 1441? As a misunderstanding, as a fool's game? Or as a superficial compromise that appeared highly artificial to everyone?

Hoffmann: It is clear that everybody read this text in his own way. Powell certainly saw in it the triumph of ambiguity, but in his eyes this was better than a fiasco. Isn't diplomacy made up of agreements that the different participants interpret in different ways? After weeks of negotiations, everybody went away convinced that he had gotten what he wanted. On the American side, one was persuaded that this resolution in no way prevented war because there was no obligation to come back to the Security Council and that the former violations by Saddam Hussein were clearly underlined; didn't one talk of a "last chance" for peace? On the other side, France considered that the text did not rule out a return to the Security Council before any resort to force, made it possible to prolong the efforts of the U.N. inspectors, and was in no way incompatible with a peaceful solution. In sum, Resolution 1441, unanimously adopted by the Security Council on November 8, 2002, after weeks of negotiations, was predictably vague enough to allow the Americans and the French to believe that their point of view had prevailed.

Until January 2003 (see ch. 1) Franco-American relations were still based on trust. Jean-David Levitte in particular remained a partner for Washington. He had published in the *New York Times* an article that one should perhaps read again with the passage of time. He said, "We are allies, we will do what we can to remain allies, but do not go too far." One was, in other words, still in a relation among allies; perhaps French diplomacy had already communicated its interpretation of the resolution, but there was not at that moment a conflict between France and the United States. One remained in ambiguity.

Bozo: But if one can suspect that the Americans staged a false U.N. overture and had in reality already decided on a military option, are not the French exposed to the opposite accusation, that of having excluded from the beginning any military intervention? It is likely that the Americans believed this.

Hoffmann: I am pretty sure that on the French side the military option had never been totally ruled out. One now knows that in December, Paris had sent a high-ranking officer to Washington to indicate to the American high command what forces the French government had decided to put at the disposal of the Americans and the British if one left some leeway to the U.N. inspectors. Chirac wanted to have some time to find out whether one could disarm Iraq without a war.

Remember that the U.N. inspectors were not particularly soft toward Saddam Hussein. On the French side, one had a great deal of respect for Hans Blix, a Scandinavian with a reputation for candor and of toughness. In Paris, one probably believed that there was some chance that the Americans, in the spirit of Resolution 1441, would take the inspections seriously and under prodding from the British, accept to grant to the inspectors a little more time. This was an illusion, because in Washington Blix was strongly distrusted. Indeed, there were attempts at discrediting him. The neoconservatives or right-wing newspapers presented him simply as Paris's man and argued that another Scandinavian, Rolf Ekeus, would have been much tougher with the Iraqis. In my understanding, the French were not only astonished to hear that for Washington the time of inspections was over, but they were also disappointed by the lack of support they had received from London. For once, the French were a bit naïve. It is true that the Americans had probably explained to the British that there was not any more time to lose, that the war could succeed only if operations were launched before the middle of March because of meteorological conditions in Iraq.

After the middle of January, the American media became more and more patriotic or chauvinistic in their tone. De Villepin's proposal to get the heads of state or government of the Big Five from the Security Council together was practically unmentioned in the press and yet the idea was not absurd. These leaders never talked directly and the chances of misunderstanding were thus increased.

Bozo: Let us come back to the style of French diplomacy. One cannot call Jacques Chirac a pacifist. He showed this in a series of brave decisions, notably in Bosnia in 1995 and in Kosovo in 1999, and yet the position he took in January 2003 on the occasion of the anniversary of the Franco-German Elysée treaty did damage his image. Repeating that war is always the worst solution—a rather good definition of pacifism—risks being understood as excluding a priori the military option. Even worse, wasn't he thus confirming America's suspicion of French complacency toward Saddam Hussein, whom Paris would have thus liked to "protect"?

Hoffmann: I too found that the formula of Jacques Chirac at that moment was unfortunate. De Villepin's speeches at the Security Council in February and March 2003 were more adept, since they stated the conditions for a resort to the use of force. These were in no way pacifist speeches. What he said was that France ruled out the military operation on the condition that the inspectors could pursue their work during a reasonable amount of time, but for afterwards he did not rule out anything. One therefore had to interpret Chirac's formula in this context: it meant that since war is always a bad solution, one had to give a last chance to peace before envisaging a military option, but I concede that the formula was perhaps ill-advised in those circumstances.

As for relations with Saddam Hussein, it is true that Chirac had met him in the 1970s, but Rumsfeld had also met him in the 1980s. There is an "Iraqi past" on the American side also. At different times, France and the United States had wanted to have good relations with Iraq. One forgets this today a little too fast.

Bozo: There remains the question of what Resolution 1441 really meant, a question which provoked the great debate of January and February 2003. Was the purpose, as the French believed, to obtain and verify the disarmament of Iraq, or was it, as the U.S. insisted, obtaining an active cooperation from Baghdad? The first interpretation allowed one to delay, the second one aimed at justifying a war.

Hoffmann: It was, obviously, quite vague. For the Americans, the behavior of the Iraqi regime conditioned the genuineness of disarmament, a position which was quite defensible. This being said, Washington would have been very disappointed to see Saddam cooperating. It would have deprived the Americans of the next step, which was their real objective: regime change. For France, the acceptance, even a reluctant one, of a precise calendar with unfettered inspections, would have proven that it was not necessary to go as far as a military operation aimed at overthrowing Saddam.

Bozo: Well, the French could have been enlightened by Colin Powell and even George Bush's statements which said, as early as October of 2002, that genuine cooperation on Saddam's part would mean in effect a regime change. Wasn't this stating clearly that one wanted much more than the simple verification of disarmament?

Hoffmann: Yes. The French should also have taken into account the frequent references in George W. Bush's entourage to the Senate resolution of 1998, which already called for regime change. The behavior of Saddam Hussein, insofar as disarmament was concerned, seemed utterly untrustworthy to the promoters of that resolution. Bush indeed had once said during the fall of 2002 that if Saddam had accepted to disarm, this would mean a regime change. All of this sheds some light on the American interpretation of Resolution 1441. The purpose was not so much to verify disarmament as to obtain a change of attitude which one knew to be unacceptable by Saddam. In any case, after February the objective of an overthrow of Iraq's regime, justified this time by the atrocities committed by Saddam in the past, prevailed in Washington and London, and public opinion was more influenced by this argument than by that of national security.

Bozo: Wasn't another French mistake to appear moving away from Resolution 1441 by suggesting that one didn't need to go beyond that, for the time being, because the potential Iraqi threat was under control, and because one could perpetuate the inspections?

Hoffmann: I did not have such an impression. France maintained its position but it was not set in concrete, if only because France was still hoping to establish a common front with the British. Were there still, at this stage, links between the American delegation at the U.N. and the French delegation? Probably not. At the end of January, Powell interpreted de Villepin's attitude, during a Security Council meeting devoted to terrorism, as a break, and from this point of view Paris perhaps made a psychological mistake. Powell was already in a difficult position in Washington and did not want to appear to have been fooled by the French. But I have already tried, in chapter 1, to explain the reasons for this hardening of France's position.

In March, at Blair's insistence, the U.S. drafted a second resolution authorizing the war, despite the inspectors' report stating that there had been some progress in Iraq's attitude. At that point, the Bush administration launched a startling public campaign of threats, pressures, and promises in order to obtain the nine votes it needed for the adoption of the resolution by the Security Council. When it became clear that those votes were not guaranteed, and that the text would probably be rejected by France and Russia, the United States withdrew the resolution, denounced the failure of the U.N., comparing it to that of the late League of Nations, and moved to war without any serious attempt at gluing the broken china. The United Nations had not been "with us," so they were "against us."

Bozo: The U.N. was not the only collateral victim in this matter; there was also NATO, paralyzed for several weeks by the confrontation between the United States and three "dissident" countries, Germany, Belgium, and France, over a rather secondary question, the question of preparations that had to be organized in order to help the defense of Turkey in case of a war with Iraq. As one was moving toward a divorce in the

Security Council, was it judicious for Paris, Brussels, and Berlin to risk another confrontation within the Atlantic Alliance? Concerning France, it risked once more appearing as the "black sheep" of the Alliance for a debatable result.

Hoffmann: Let us not reverse the responsibility. It was the Americans who knowingly used this affair to test the "loyalty" of the NATO allies by asking for help for Turkey in a very hypothetical case, in which its own loyalty to Washington would lead to military reactions in Baghdad. Turkey itself wasn't asking for that much. France and Germany, as well as Belgium, had said "no" in the Atlantic Council. The compromise accepted by the Germans consisted in resorting to the military committee of which France is not a member, but of course all of this was exploited by Washington and provoked the wrath of Donald Rumsfeld. As a consequence there has been no more talk of NATO, and Turkey rejected the bounty that Washington proposed in exchange for having American military forces receive the right to open a second front in Iraq by using Turkey as a base. The American military have profoundly regretted this fiasco. A little later Paul Wolfowitz himself publicly criticized the Turkish government, asked it to admit the seriousness of its mistakes, and the great champion of democracy in the Middle East expressed his regret that the Turkish army had failed to exert greater pressure on the newly elected Turkish parliament.

Bozo: I concede that there was an American provocation in the NATO affair, but one can ask the same question, mutatis mutandis, concerning the European Union (EU), whose ambition to have a common foreign and security policy—let us not even talk of a common defense—broke on the shoals of the Iraqi conflict. The United States is not a member of the EU, and in this affair the mistakes are European, even if

Washington obviously exploited the situation. Here French diplomacy has an obvious responsibility. Did it need to present the Franco-German position as having to be that of the whole of the EU before scolding the applicants for membership, because their opinion did not correspond to what the French hoped it would be? One finds again this old French failure to understand the aspirations of that part of Europe which has been liberated from communism and wants to be close to the United States, in which it sees, rightly or wrongly, its liberator at the end of the Cold War. It is, after all, a historically explainable and legitimate aspiration. Was there a better service one could perform for the Bush administration, for whom it became easy thereafter to rally the "new Europe" against the old one?

Hoffmann: The European Union has played no important role in this story. Neither Chirac nor Blair have ever invoked Europe; they have talked about the U.N. and Europe was in such a state of division that it would not have been very clever to underline it. Either one leans on the United States, or else one leans on a certain idea of the U.N., but at that moment there was no Europe.

Among the Italian and Spanish rulers, irritation toward the German and French "governesses" was visible. The other relatively important countries were furious to be placed at the same level as Luxemburg; the Americans have cleverly exploited that feeling. They, along with Blair, launched an offensive of division of the EU in obtaining the signature of a statement in support of the United States by the leaders of many "old" members and by the leaders of most of the future East European members. Thus, the attempt to define a common foreign and military policy for the European Union, which had begun in 1998, rapidly collapsed. Between France and the applicant states, which had already taken part in the constitutional work of the convention presided over by Valéry Giscard d'Estaing, there was indeed a complete misunderstanding, but one has to recognize that in the short run these countries were not yet part of the European diplomatic game. What was important in the immediate term was the mobilization of the existing EU of the Fifteen, even if it was not very clever to tell the Poles to shut up. In the end, and despite the skill of Javier Solana, it was obvious that the Union was not an actor on the international diplomatic and strategic stage, and that the United States absolutely refused to let it be one.

To come back to the United States and to conclude on that period, I would stress that the attitude of the American leaders can be explained to a large extent by the support of public opinion. After September 11 there was the rebirth of a wounded and indignant patriotism, a rallying behind the president who promised a decisive victory, had taken a hard line, and offered firm leadership. Thus opinion came to accept the arguments linking Iraq to terrorism, and the media put themselves at the service of the administration and of the public. Tocqueville would not have been surprised. For a country half of whose voters do not vote, and for whom politics is not the condition of their lives, it takes a major crisis and a president who presents himself as a savior to get a public mobilization.

5

GULLIVER UNBOUND

Bozo: Let us get to the war itself. How do you explain its popularity in a public opinion which was at first more worried than really enthusiastic and whose deep divisions were revealed by the public opinion polls (40 percent for, 40 percent only on condition of a legitimation by the U.N., 20 percent against)?

Hoffmann: Wars in the United States are popular when they are presented in simple terms and on two levels: national security and American ideals, in other words, survival and a certain messianic idealism. In this case it worked perfectly. Concerning national security, Bush and his administration exploited the "shock and awe" created by September 11, they explained that Saddam Hussein's arsenal posed a very serious threat to the nation, and exploited the idea that there existed a link between Saddam and the terrorists of al Qaeda and the Middle East. Half of Americans ended up believing that Iraqis had been deeply implicated in the hijacking of airplanes on September 11, whereas in reality it was Saudis and Egyptians.

On the second level Bush opened the doors of humanitarianism and described in classic terms the crimes of the Iraqi regime, which were indeed horrendous. Thus, it was necessary to liberate the victims and promote democracy in this part of the world. All of this was in conformity with the American style and principles that I analyzed almost forty years ago during the Vietnam War in my book *Gulliver's Troubles* (1968). The cause was just, the Americans presented themselves both as defenders of their threatened fatherland and as reformers of world order, they mixed once more a nationalism which didn't recognize itself as such and good intentions that nobody except freedom haters could put in doubt. The media, which had recovered from the shock of Vietnam, fed this fever with analyses which were often simplistic, often ignorant of the outside world, but also chauvinistic or delirious with naïve idealism. Success in Afghanistan had prepared the ground.

Bozo: You have been much concerned with the problem of ethics in international affairs. Leaving aside the problem of the legality of this intervention and the question of weapons of mass destruction—the official justification of the war—this military victory which was apparently easy and almost painless for the Americans, the fact that a bloody regime had been overthrown, doesn't this justify intervention by giving it after the fact an undeniable legitimacy?

Hoffmann: If one follows the most widely accepted approach, that of the just war theory, there are two main elements which concern the *jus ad bellum*: under what conditions is the resort to war just, and the *jus in bello*: what are the appropriate means? On the first point, as long as one limited oneself to the problem of weapons of mass destruction, which were supposed to be in the hands of a barbaric regime, one could answer yes, the conditions of a just cause are met. On the second point, that of means, one must recognize that, thanks to precision weapons, there was a considerable effort to limit the number of civilian victims, as indeed already in 1991, and for avoiding the destruction of all the infrastructures of life which were still a casualty in 1991. However, one would have to know the number of Iraqi victims and this will probably never be the case.

This leaves us nevertheless with those difficult questions concerning the *jus ad bellum*. First of all, the problem of intentions: they have to be just. But what were those intentions? To liberate the Iraqis? To extend America's power? To fight against an aggression? To impose respect to commitments to the U.N. undertaken by Iraq? It isn't very clear. Secondly, there is the problem of last resort. Could one convincingly argue that the containment of Saddam's alleged arsenal had failed and that preventive action was therefore necessary? Moreover, there is the problem of authorization, a question which is particularly important because of the difficulty of defining the intentions which are no longer, as in the Middle Ages, those of a prince who is supposed to be a good Christian, but those of a group of quite diverse decision makers. Indeed, authorization has as much importance as a just cause—states almost always find a just cause to put forward—and is as important as intentions. This is why authorization has to be given by a legitimate authority which approves the military action. Hence the question of whether there shouldn't have been an international authorization. In fact, the whole doctrine of just war needs to be thoroughly renovated in order to take into account international relations in the twenty-first century.

Bozo: When one talks of international legitimation, does one necessarily mean a clear and firm statement of the Security

Council? After all, in Kosovo in 1999 it did not come, and countries such as France accepted that fact.

Hoffmann: Yes, but the conditions were quite different, in the sense that at the time it was clear that there would be a Russian veto in the Security Council. Indeed, the U.S. and the allies didn't want to go through the Security Council in order to preserve a future with the Russians. One knew that they would veto a resolution and one was convinced that if there was a confrontation it would be good for no one. Finally, once the war was launched by NATO, there was at the U.N. a resolution submitted to the Security Council which condemned NATO's intervention and it was rejected by a large majority; Kofi Annan stated that he understood and did not condemn this intervention. In other words, the situation was very different from the present case. This time, there had been long periods of discussion and the famous second resolution had to be withdrawn. Let me add that in 1999 the allies' calculation was correct, since the Russians ended up by abandoning Milošević and rejoining the coalition.

Bozo: Concerning legitimacy, the question is less that of the existence of a formal mandate than that of the sincerity in the quest for such a mandate.

Hoffmann: Yes, indeed, especially as the last resolution, 1441, was not considered by most of the Security Council members as decisive, i.e., as constituting a mandate for war.

There remains the problem which, in my eyes, is the most difficult, i.e., regime change as an objective. Overthrowing an awful tyrant is, in the first analysis, a just cause. But this is not the one that Bush had put forward.

Bozo: Can one justify an intervention solely on the basis of a regime's nature and of its misdeeds? Wouldn't this approach have avoided many debates and divisions, especially as this was a much less debatable fact than the existence of weapons of mass destruction in Iraq? Was it possible under the charter of the U.N.?

Hoffmann: The Saddam Hussein case posed extremely difficult questions about international intervention against regimes that are engaged in ferocious policies of repression. One has to recognize that on this point international law, which is still founded on nonintervention and state sovereignty, is not satisfactory, and that the humanitarian interventions legitimized by the United Nations in the last ten years have been so in a limited way only. In 1991, Saddam crushed in the most brutal and public way the Kurds and the Shi'ites, whom the United States had called upon to revolt. Immediately after the Gulf War, the United States obtained from the U.N. a collective intervention in order to protect the Kurds from new massacres, which made the autonomy of the Kurdish part of Iraq possible. Then came the intervention to put an end to chaos in Somalia—it failed—then in order to prevent, belatedly, ethnic massacres in Bosnia, Kosovo, and East Timor. There was no intervention in the genocide in Rwanda, and neither the U.S. nor the U.N., as I have stated, behaved honorably. Thus it is not without difficulty that a new norm was established: the possibility of a collective intervention against a government that perpetrates serious violations of human rights, especially when those violations threaten international or regional peace and security.

But please note that in none of these cases was there any question of regime change. To reduce a state's sovereignty by collective action aimed at putting an end to a government's violation of human rights is one thing; to overthrow the government by force and to replace it with a regime that is more acceptable to those who intervene constitutes a much more radical assault on sovereignty. The United States was passive when Saddam Hussein used chemical weapons against the Kurds at the beginning of the 1980s and when he massacred Shi'ites in great numbers in 1991. It never presented at the time to the U.N. the problem of regime change necessitated by Iraq's violations of human rights. One should have done it in 1991, but how many members of the coalition would have supported Washington? The team of George Bush the father after the Gulf War had hoped for or expected the fall of the defeated regime due to internal upheavals. This did not occur and indeed, the success of the repression of the Kurdish and Shi'ite rebellions consolidated Saddam Hussein's power.

The fact remains that the problem of humanitarian intervention to overthrow a regime is now clearly on the agenda and will not be avoidable in the future. However, it will be difficult for the United Nations to give a satisfactory answer. Too many members of the organization have bloody regimes and the representatives of these states will do all they can to block any proposal for a collective military intervention. I will come back to this point later.

Would regime change have been more acceptable as a war aim than the elimination of weapons of mass destruction? I don't think so (nor did one of the main protagonists of the war, Paul Wolfowitz). It would have required the establishment of a double principle: on the one hand, the principle that one can indeed change a regime if it commits extreme brutalities and on the other hand that this can be done retroactively. I don't think that the majority of the members of the Security Council would have followed. The problem is indeed that of knowing how far humanitarian law goes, and since one has proceeded up to now on a case-by-case basis, it remains very vague. How many states would have accepted moving from an intervention that does not overthrow a criminal government to an intervention that proclaims that this government is so awful that it has to be replaced?

Bozo: Let us come back to the weapons of mass destruction, the main justification for intervention. The fact that so many questions have been raised about this argument, and that the coalition did not find any such weapons shouldn't, I think, lead one to bury this debate. Independently of the specific case of Iraq, the problem of the legitimacy of the doctrine of preemption is raised, whether one wants it or not. What is your viewpoint? Can such a doctrine be justified? Under what conditions? In what framework?

Hoffmann: The nuclear problem has been placed in the front lines by the new American strategic doctrine. According to this doctrine, weapons of mass destruction in hostile hands have become a potential casus belli. With this argument, the team of George Bush defends the notion of preventive action. This approach, in my eyes, is dangerous. If it is understandable and perhaps even necessary against terrorists who cannot be deterred, it is much less acceptable against states, in addition to the fact that it obviously violates the U.N. charter. A preventive, unilateral action of the United States against states that try to obtain a nuclear arsenal would only encourage other states to do the same in order to protect themselves against their alleged enemies: another recipe for turning the world into a jungle. This strategy even risks inciting some countries to support and arm terrorists, which had not been the case with Saddam. It is better to proceed case by case and multilaterally.

Bozo: We have deviated a little in this chapter in which we were going to discuss the war itself. You have written and talked a great deal about war; your course on war at Harvard has been one of the most popular. Since the Gulf War in 1991, one explains that whatever war is taking place at a given moment—Kuwait, Bosnia, Kosovo, Afghanistan—constitutes a revolution in the military arts, particularly because of the precision and efficiency of strikes, their "cleanness," etc. How do you view this last conflict? What novelties, particularly in the military or technological domain, did you find in it?

Hoffmann: In many respects, contrary to what happened in the first Gulf War, strikes occurred with great precision. Nothing happened this time that was comparable to the destruction in 1991 of shelters that had been deemed to be for military use and yet were occupied by civilians. Operations this time were much better prepared. To be sure, the beginning of the war was marked by a great deal of improvisation, because the Americans had learned that Saddam Hussein was at a specific place, which was immediately bombarded. The information was actually false, but this episode showed the astonishing progress that has occurred in finding targets and in hitting them with precision. Coordination of air and ground forces has been much more efficient than before, which is of great interest for future wars.

As a result, the striking power of the American forces—air force, tanks, and artillery combined—and the skill of British forces defeated in twenty-three days an Iraqi army which had practically abandoned the battlefield to the steamroller of the enemy. The Iraqi army was disorganized by a lightning progression that it did not expect. There was no sign of defensive planning, there was a retreat without real fighting, there was no strategy of scorched earth. Everything happened as if the Iraqis had been taken by surprise by the decision of Tommy Franks, the commander-in-chief of the Anglo-American forces, to begin the ground war at the same time as the air war—unlike in 1991. We now know that the Iraqi forces were largely left to themselves and that the orders they received—when they received them at all—were contradictory. Thus, the Anglo-American victory was obviously helped by the state of the Iraqi troops—exhausted by years of war, weakened by a decade of embargoes, and mediocrely equipped. As a result, the transformation of Baghdad into Stalingrad was not even attempted, fortunately for the civilians who would have otherwise been massacred.

Bozo: From the point of view of strategy or doctrine, how do you appreciate the abandonment of the Powell doctrine, according to which America should resort to force only if it has at its disposal overwhelming superiority and a well-defined exit strategy? The civilians at the Pentagon, who seem to have had unprecedented influence on the preparation of events, must be able to congratulate themselves on having broken this taboo by planning an operation which was much more mobile and less heavy and, in a sense, more daring.

Hoffmann: Yes, that was a break with the Powell doctrine, but one has to understand that this was mainly a political doctrine concerning the conditions under which the use of force should be envisaged. This time, the political parameters were not the same; once one shifted to an international policy that was much more offensive and in which the resort to the military tool had a much larger role, a challenge to the Powell doctrine was almost ipso facto in the works. As for the superiority and the certainty of victory demanded by the Powell doctrine, one was assured of the second but one probably didn't have the first. It is true that mobility and far superior armaments compensate for the relative lack of numbers. It is also true that there was no exit strategy, which Powell had called for, but there was no problem of exit, at least in the short term, since occupation was a major part of the strategy. . . .

Bozo: During those few days when one had an impression of a slowdown, very sharp criticisms were made by the military concerning the planning of operations. What did they mean in terms of relations between civilians and military in this administration? Moreover, wasn't there in this open break with the Powell doctrine, a deliberate message directed at the intentions of potential adversaries, which consists in saying, we will always be in a position to act militarily if we need to do so; in other words, war will always be an option?

Hoffmann: In this administration relations between the military and the civilians have not necessarily been very good, and the war has illustrated it. The generals obviously considered that, by planning a war with relatively small forces, the civilians were obliging the military to accept excessive risks, and they did not like this. It would indeed be interesting to know what Powell himself thought about that side of things.

As for the message addressed to eventual adversaries, it was undeniable. It is in a sense an aspect of deterrence. But I am sure that it reflected above all an absolute confidence in the possibility of using force in a way which would be reasonably acceptable by delicate souls and a conviction according to which preventive action must be much more frequent than before. Therefore, when one intervenes somewhere, one must not commit all one's forces in this case. On this point, which is essential to him, Rumsfeld is the anti-Powell.

Bozo: What are the possible strategic effects of this openly demonstrated military and technological superiority and obvious determination to use it? You seem to doubt that it would have as genuine a deterrent effect on potential adversaries. Do you fear, inversely, that it will encourage them to find compensation on another ground, that of terrorism, or the search for weapons of mass destruction, and, in the meantime, of guerillas in Iraq?

Hoffmann: I am not sure there is a single answer. Concerning terrorist groups, they are obviously encouraged to continue engaging in terrorism; for them, it is the only way of establishing a balance, by undermining America's superiority from below. For others, i.e., state actors, America's military and technological superiority will perhaps have a deterrent effect on some, but not on others; see North Korea and to some extent Iran, as compared to Libya. For the rest, it is difficult to know what the attitude of countries like Russia and China will be if America's use of force becomes systematic. Will it be seen as an invitation to restraint or as an encouragement to escalation? On the American side there is a message that consists in saying, if you annoy us too much you are dead. This is part of this new game which is not deterrence. But to what extent have adversaries already taken it into account and prepared the next gambit? It is too soon to say. America's hesitations toward North Korea are significant; Bush explained that because North Korea has nuclear weapons, negotiation is necessary. Nevertheless, the administration is divided: the allies of the United States prefer soft handling, but the official goal of the negotiations that have begun remains the voluntary demilitarization of Pyongyang. Nothing is simple, and nothing has been decided.

Bozo: Let us move now to the question of the media coverage, an essential component of any conflict. Here too one is struck by a radical innovation, which is dangerously effective: the status of "embedded journalists," which was offered to and adopted by the journalists, and has mainly benefited the Anglo-American war machine, since those who are embedded naturally adhere to the institution and its discourse. As for the others, the "independents," in fact they found themselves dependent on coalition forces for their security, which a priori did not increase their sense of critical journalism.

Hoffmann: Embeddedness has been a remarkably skillful policy, very different from that of the first Gulf War when the Pentagon had tried to keep the journalists far from the front lines. This time, the decision to incorporate the journalists into military units has had a double effect: the correspondents have made common cause with the fighters, and saw themselves as soldiers; and each unit could only see a small side of the battlefield, and was deprived of any global vision. As for the independent journalists, they found it indeed quite difficult to remain so, since they had no access to any interesting sources of information, and found themselves in dangerous positions in battle. This has led, in the media, to a sometimes nauseating triumphalism.

A comparison with the British is pretty depressing. They have not let their critical sense shrink for a second, whereas American journalists who were embedded let themselves be sometimes bamboozled, as in the unfortunate episode of this young American military woman, wounded and taken captive by Iraqis; her liberation seems to have been largely staged by the movie services of the Pentagon. The funniest part is that it was the British who discovered the subterfuge.

I also think—this is not an excuse but perhaps an explanation—that the journalists had been so frustrated by the experience of the first Gulf War that they accepted without protest a system which offered permanent contact with coalition forces, and that the comparison with the experience of Vietnam, during which the press showed itself much more aggressive, is debatable because of the time factor. Let us not forget that the Vietnam War lasted ten years. Those long years helped reawaken the critical sense of the press. The real lesson one can draw from the comparison is that when officialdom wants to put the media into its pocket, it can do so, but on condition of winning quickly.

Bozo: Indeed, one is struck by the difference between British and American media coverage. The polemic between the BBC and the British government, dramatized by the Kelly affair, has been instructive in this respect.

Hoffmann: Yes, there have been two different ethics. Some—even the BBC, which is after all an organ of the state—acted with the idea that they are at the service of truth, for the public's interests, and the Americans had a certain tendency to see themselves as a fourth power, which is quite different. The Kelly affair—the suicide of this specialist of the secret services who had complained to a BBC journalist about the pressures he was under to dramatize the case against Iraq—has shaken Tony Blair's government. There hasn't been anything comparable in Washington; no serious investigation was undertaken by Congress, which the Republicans control, until much later, and there hasn't been any resort to an independent judge.

I repeat, during the war in Iraq, the BBC preferred truth to propaganda, was scrupulous in its presentation of the facts, and therefore contributed more to the prestige of Britain than the American programs which sometimes gave the impression of trying to "sell" America. This had already been the case when I listened to the BBC, and not to the Voice of America, as an adolescent in occupied France.

When one looks at CNN and at the BBC, one has the feeling of watching two different wars. In the United States supporting the troops meant supporting the war. This is totally different and is perhaps due to the fact that in America big wars are more popular wars than in a country such as England, which has an old experience of a professional army and a tradition in which the media's honor consists in being critical. In the last analysis, there was no counterweight in America.

I don't mean to say that it was impossible to express reservations or dissent in the press or on television. Like Tony Judt, I have been able to do so on the respected television program of Charlie Rose. But faced with radio stations of appalling chauvinism and the epic vulgarity of the Fox television network, neither CNN nor the *Washington Post* dared go beyond a saddening conformity and, while the *New York Times* had some room for critical articles, they were accompanied by anti-French polemics.

6

AFTER THE WAR

The Beginning (April 2003–September 2003)

Bozo: Let's talk about the immediate situation after the war. As one could have expected, the conflict was over quickly and the Anglo-American victory uncontestable. But if the war took place exactly as the strategists at the Pentagon had predicted, this was not true afterward as the problems of the occupation, beginning with that of security, and then the difficulties of reconstruction, in particular that of a political system. These problems and difficulties have made it clear that, despite George Bush's grand appearance on an aircraft carrier to announce the end of military operations, the end was far from over. Wasn't there a lack of planning for after the war?

Hoffmann: This was indeed the case. As soon as their victory was achieved, the GIs tried to turn themselves into soldiers of peace and the gap in planning for the postwar became blindingly apparent. It would be incorrect to say that the Americans had not prepared anything. But the working groups that the State Department had constituted have had no influence, for several rather appalling reasons. On the one hand, the Iraqi exiles and especially Mr. Chalabi, who was the favorite of the Pentagon civilians, had promised the Americans that much of the army and police of Saddam Hussein would change sides, as the Italians had in 1943, and furthermore that vast clandestine forces were ready to take over the maintenance of security. "Don't worry," they said to the Americans, "you shall be greeted as liberators. It is not necessary to mobilize twenty or thirty thousand more soldiers." In any case, the military were unenthusiastic at the idea that they would be utilized for police functions, which was absolutely not what they had been trained for. On the other hand, even if there had been efforts to prepare the postwar situation, these efforts were handicapped by the disagreements between the State Department and the Defense Department, hence a genuine cacophony. The Pentagon civilians prevailed, adopted the idea of their clients, the exiles who wanted the liquidation of Saddam's army and the sacking of his bureaucracy, which left a void both for security and for reconstruction. Let us take the problem of looting. The Americans saw to it that the oil fields would be guarded, but why did they remain indifferent to all the other scenes of looting? A good number of curators of American and European museums had immediately launched an appeal to prevent the looting of the Iraqi museums. They were not listened to and the looting took place with the occupation forces looking on. This has had a disastrous effect on the morale of the Iraqis. The economic effects have been incalculable and have delayed the return to a more normal situation.

If the overthrow of the regime was a relatively easy thing, the restoration of order was much more difficult. The Americans knew how to plan for military operations with great care

urban Iraqi, insecurity, unknown under Saddam, has continued. Secondly, American forces have been subjected to two kinds of attacks: the number of deaths since the end of operations has far exceeded that of soldiers killed during the military operations; also, there have been spectacular attacks against oil fields and pipelines, against the headquarters of the United Nations, against the main Shi'ite mosques, etc., etc. The objective of those attacks was less to kill people than to increase insecurity and to delay the process of economic reconstruction of the country. They have often been attributed to infiltrations of terrorists, al Qaeda or groups affiliated with al Qaeda, but there have also been attacks by Iraqi civilians, exasperated by the often brutal control exerted by American soldiers. Thus one got to an absurd situation: war had been declared in the name of the world struggle against terrorism, and victory has favored the installation of terrorism in Iraq.

I must repeat: the confusion has not been only over the material issues but also over politics. Was it necessary to begin by imposing almost total American and British control over the country in order to purge the Ba'athists, including in the police and administration? Wouldn't it have been better to awaken quickly new political forces, beginning at the local level, so that it would have been Iraqis recruiting an Iraqi police force for the urgent tasks such as security and the fight against terrorists? While those political forces got organized, should one have given broad leeway to the Iraqis, or should one have warned them against giving any power to Shi'ite Islamists or to the former leaders of tribes? Some, it is well known, have evoked the German and Japanese precedents of 1945 but the resemblances are few; there was neither a homogeneous and docile population, as in Japan, nor were there liberal, socialist, and Catholic traditions, which had played an important role in Germany in the nineteenth century, and dominated under the Weimar Republic. Iraq is a country where political life had been totally repressed, where relations between the Shi'ites—the majority of the population whom Saddam had oppressed—and the Sunni, who were in a minority and whom Saddam had favored, were extremely tense; where the Kurds had, since 1991, succeeded in acquiring an almost complete autonomy with a sort of two-party system but only thanks to America's protection. Finally, there were the exiles, financed and used by the Pentagon and security agencies. The first American administrator, retired General Jay Garner, whom the Pentagon had chosen, had supported the exiles, talked about a provisional government, and held a few preparatory meetings, but in a rather confused manner. Above all, in the face of events, he did not seem to have sufficient weight. Hence his replacement in May 2003 by a diplomat, Paul Bremer, a former aide to Henry Kissinger, who was acceptable both to the State Department, which had been quite frustrated under Garner, and to the Pentagon, but he had no experience in the Arab world. His arrival meant a kind of recapture of control, priority for problems of security in daily life, and extreme reliance (which reminded me of Mr. McNamara in the Vietnam days) on statistics of material progress and a postponement of political renewal. He also made the mistake of demobilizing Iraq's army and of purging the Ba'athist administration, which deprived the Americans of their collaboration for the maintenance of security and order and alienated hundreds of thousands of Saddam's employees, now deprived of any salary. There has been, of course, the constitution of the interim governmental authority, but it has had very little authority. It was kept on a short leash by its American protectors; it was deeply divided; it had a small majority of former exiles; and it was not capable of obtaining the U.N.'s blessing.

Bozo: Wasn't it, however, the beginning of a possible virtuous circle? After all, nobody could seriously imagine that in a few months Iraq would return to a kind of normalcy, without even talking about genuine democratization.

Hoffmann: I doubt it. There has been an awakening of awareness of the situation in the United States, both in opinion and in the media; members of Congress have worried greatly about security issues and, above all, about the cost the president finally announced: $87 billion for Iraq and Afghanistan, $67 billion of which were for the armed struggle. The Pentagon has asked for the sending to Iraq of additional forces, which would make the American army capable of altogether preserving security in the cities, chasing the terrorists, protecting the borders, and serving as a police and battle force. But Rumsfeld has obstinately refused. Was it because he didn't want the armed forces to get bogged down in a new Vietnam? Or was it because he wanted to keep substantial forces for other possible conflicts? Was it in order to insure that his gamble about "slimming down" the mammoth American army could be won? The military around him could grumble, but did not dare contradict him. Congress, which of course has been thinking about the elections of 2004, doesn't like sending more troops either, on the whole. Under those conditions, what is there to be done? The solution, which some have mentioned, of attempting aggressively to hire and train police forces and a new Iraqi army is far from being effective. Would not this have meant, as usual, giving priority to the urgent over the long term, which is the reconstitution of an Iraqi authority that would control these forces? However, in the absence of such an authority, they would inevitably be placed under American and British command and treated as the coalition's auxiliaries by many Iraqis. To resolve in such a way the numerical problem of forces—on paper and for how much time—without any motion on the political ground was not really satisfactory. The political problem has still not been solved; the Sunnis have been hostile, the Shi'ites have been divided between pro-Americans and a young Islamist clergy which rejects the occupation.

As for the other frequently mentioned idea of calling on new members for the coalition, such as India, Thailand, Turkey, France, Germany, etc., it raises two major problems. From a strictly military viewpoint, the American high command and also Rumsfeld were not very well disposed; it would have complicated the exercise of command, confronting again, as in Kosovo, the difficulties characteristic of coalitions, and diluted the authority of the American high commanders. Finally and above all, some of the eventual partners made it clear that in exchange for the "right" of sharing with the present coalition the losses and the expenses, they wanted a resolution from the Security Council which would have enlarged the role of the United Nations and defined the framework of this new coalition, indicated its objectives, and given the U.N. a right of supervision (Kofi Annan did not ask for more; he did not want to send blue-helmeted soldiers into a war zone, but he didn't want less either). This has for a long time been unacceptable to American hawks, who have not forgotten the confusion of the double chain of command (the U.N. and the U.S.) in Bosnia, and above all do not want to appear to capitulate before an organization which did not support them at the decisive moment, an organization which they deplore. Colin Powell, on whom all difficult tasks are pushed, has tried to find a compromise formula, with the agreement of the president. But once again France was particularly reluctant and asked for a primary role—to be defined—for the U.N., a return, so to speak, to international legitimacy. In any case, an enlargement of the coalition meant complicating the work of the Anglo-American authority which the Security Council has recognized but not legitimized, and it meant multiplying targets for terrorists, who saw enemies in the partners of the Americans and did not hesitate to kill their representatives and those of the U.N. even when they were engaged in humanitarian work; this was probably a memory of the bitter years of sanctions inflicted on Iraq by the United Nations.

In fact, American diplomats have, since the fall of 2003, looked for a squaring of the circle: the creation of a multinational force, of a broader coalition sponsored by the U.N. but under American command. This meant the continuation of the effective power of the present governing authority, with a legitimation by the U.N. which it has not been possible to achieve. Indeed, the main obstacle to the success of this attempt was Bush himself, supported by Dick Cheney and Donald Rumsfeld. He continued imperturbably to speak about a universal war against terrorism, to call for total victory, and to make of Iraq the central battlefield in this struggle. In order to invite other countries to cooperate with the coalition within the framework of the U.N. and for the good of the Iraqis, he has summoned these countries to participate, in the interest of humankind, in this struggle and in the sharing of burdens with the United States, but not in the sharing of responsibilities. In my opinion, if American forces are not increased, it is evident that sooner or later they will have to be relieved of everything which is not the restoration of security, and to accept a return to the U.N. both in order to facilitate nation-building, i.e., reconstruction, an area in which the U.N. has long experience, and above all to revive political life in a country which has never had one. It is not a dubious coalition which is best placed for the promotion of democracy and liberalism. Some time ago, there had been a failed "Vietnamization"; what was needed now was an "Iraqization" under international guidance.

Bozo: One could have hoped that after the war Franco-American difficulties over Iraq would get much less acute. This happened during a few months, with the French being relatively prudent in their commentaries and not showing any *Schadenfreude* when the coalition got into trouble. But difficulties started again in September 2003 when the United States introduced a new resolution aimed at enlarging the coalition. This time there was no question of a veto, but was it necessary once again to complicate America's task?

Hoffmann: It is true that there was a new conflict with France, both over a new role for the U.N. and over that of the occupiers. The reality is that Americans began to understand that whether they were legitimized by the U.N. or not, the new international forces that might be sent in order to improve security would be a very weak supplement (nobody in the Congress and in the media asked why countries which were not favorable to the war would send their soldiers to their deaths and would want to pay for the coalition's errors). Thus the real problem is that which France has posed. If the violence that followed the end of the war results from the occupation and from hostility to the occupiers, wasn't it necessary to put an end to this occupation quite quickly and to transfer the political and reconstruction powers to the Iraqis under U.N. control?

One may want to criticize the French position over deadlines and methods. Could one really transfer these powers in a few weeks? For a return to political life, wasn't it better to begin at the ground level, even if a symbolic transfer on top was useful? But what once again reawakened anti-French statements in the media (Thomas Friedman in the *New York Times* decided that France was an "enemy country"), and also in the State Department, was the fact that France wished that the nonmilitary power exerted by Mr. Bremer and by the occupiers be transferred as quickly as possible to the U.N. and to the Iraqis. For many Americans who did not think that it was the occupation that increased insecurity, or who felt that only the occupiers should decide both the speed and the shape of a transfer of powers to the Iraqis, France simply was trying to deprive the Americans of their victory. However, the so-called anti-American position of France was the same as that of former president Carter! In reality, one observes an interesting reversal of positions. France, which in the beginning had been very unenthusiastic about the Iraqi governmental council, came out for a symbolic transfer of Iraqi sovereignty to it, and it was the Americans who opposed it by arguing that this council had no democratic legitimacy! At one point, to make matters even more bizarre, it was the American protégé Mr. Chalabi, who adopted a position closer to France's than to the American one. The fact is that the Americans wanted to wage a policy of democratization under their control and even the exiles have found this hard to bear.

Bozo: Let us come to the postwar problems beyond Iraq. Just after the coalition's victory, the question that was rightly asked was: "Whose turn is it now?" Success in Iraq seemed to make the hypothesis of a sequel credible. If one restricts oneself to the axis of evil, would it be Iran first, or North Korea first, or would it be Syria, which Washington threatened as soon as the conflict was over? Do you think that there are among America's plans the project of a fight with a country other than Iraq? Which one? By which method? Have the events that have occurred since then, and the difficulties that had to be faced after the war, had an influence on this possible program?

Hoffmann: I do not believe that the Bush administration is now preparing other plans of attack, but I don't doubt that there are other projects in the files at the Pentagon. In my opinion, nothing will happen for a while because everybody will be waiting. If the number of assaults diminishes, if Iraq seems to become more peaceful, if opposition is limited to that part of Iraq which was the base of Saddam's power, there will not be automatic consequences that one could foresee. However, the real risk is that some would like to attack the neighbors of Iraq who "feed terrorism."

Bozo: How does the case of the other two countries on the list of the "Axis of Evil," North Korea and Iran, look, comparatively? Concerning North Korea, what was striking, even before the war in Iraq, was the American will to differentiate it from Iraq.

Hoffmann: Let us begin with Iran. What would stop the Americans much more than in the case of Iraq is the fact that an intervention would be totally counterproductive, given the existence of a real democratic movement among young Iranians. It would be better if one could not later accuse the United States of having, through its intervention, sunk a revolution that was in the making.

Korea is really a completely different problem. The Americans agree that negotiations will have to take place with the strict agreement of South Korea, Japan, China, and Russia, and it is not here a problem of choosing between unilateralism and multilateralism. They are incapable of acting alone and the mediating role of China is indispensable. This being said, the administration is divided between hard-liners and less hard-liners. There are many questions. Should one negotiate or not? The answer until now is yes, but with whom? Only North Korea, as Pyongyang seemed to prefer, or also Russia, China, South Korea, and Japan, as Pyongyang has ended up accepting? With what purposes? The liquidation of the nuclear program, or an agreement which, in exchange for such a liquidation and for intrusive inspections, would calm Pyongyang's fears concerning an American attack and would offer food to the North Koreans? The reason given for explaining the difference in treatment with Iraq is the vulnerability of South Korea to nuclear aggression or an invasion from the north. But the Bush administration is divided between those who, having negotiated under the Clinton presidency with Pyongyang, believe that there are interests that can be reconciled, and the neoconservatives who believe that North Korea is irrational, totally unpredictable and dangerous. Can one really deter a madman who wants to play the game of Samson and Delilah? Therefore if multilateral negotiations fail, preventive war would be a temptation for many.

Bozo: There is a supplementary element: the allies of the United States, i.e., South Korea and Japan have much greater weight finally on this issue than the Europeans had in the Iraqi case, because they are more vulnerable.

Hoffmann: Right. They weigh more by the simple fact that there are only two of them; the Europeans, well one never knows which ones one is talking about.

Bozo: Wouldn't this be an opportunity for the Europeans to try to refloat the U.N.? In this case, the United States is in need of multilateralism. The Korean question became a U.N. question a few months ago, when the International Atomic Energy Agency presented its conclusions to the Security Council. Do you think the Americans are ready, in this instance, to play the game of the United Nations?

Hoffmann: Yes, insofar as South Korea and Japan want to implicate the U.N. Unfortunately, one doesn't know too well what could come out of the U.N., which is why the Americans have been so ambivalent, and they remain so. Concerning Iran, the IAEA has exerted very strong pressure on Teheran: this both covers and serves Washington.

Bozo: Let us move on to the Middle East. Since the beginning of this crisis, two logics are in confrontation. There is a European, and in any event French, logic, according to which the real priority in the area is the resolution of the Israeli-Palestinian conflict, a conflict which the war in Iraq can only worsen; and then there is an American logic, according to which "dealing with" Iraq, as one called it in Washington, would help resolve the Israeli-Palestinian problem. A similar debate had already taken place in 1991 and it is true that events in Kuwait had a favorable effect since they led to the Madrid process and then to Oslo, because the administration of the first Bush was eager after the war to show that it was ready to do what was needed to resolve this problem, even if it meant very strong pressure on Israel. Can one compare these two moments, 1991 and 2003? Are there reasons to believe that Bush the son wants to show that he is also capable of obtaining peace by getting involved and by imposing concessions on all parties, including the Israelis?

Hoffmann: It is not easy to answer. It is clear that Colin Powell, the State Department and the British would like this to be the case, but what goes on in Bush's own head isn't very clear, nor is it clear whether what will dominate in the perspective of the 2004 election campaign is domestic politics or foreign policy. If it were foreign policy, he would have followed his own road map, i.e., exerted pressure on both parties, Israel and the Palestinians, but by constantly reminding us that his main priority is war against terrorism, he very much limits pressure on Israel and forces the Palestinians to bear the full responsibility for acts of violence. He orders them to disarm the terrorist factions, in other words, to attack people who are much better armed and more popular, especially in Gaza, than the poor Palestinian authority. The Palestinian government, already constrained by Arafat and battered by Sharon, has no interest in risking a civil war and its own defeat. Sharon, if he follows the road map, runs fewer risks. Israeli opinion does not support Jewish settlements in the occupied territories with great enthusiasm and, anyhow, dismantling them is envisaged only for much later, except in the case of Gaza. On the other hand, if Bush has his eyes set on domestic policy and terrorism goes on, it is likely he will say that if the road map has failed, it's the Palestinians's fault. When in 2004 he endorsed Sharon's unilateral plan of withdrawal from some of Gaza and only a few West Bank settlements by arguing that one had to accept realistically changes on the ground, he undermined the road map, which assumed not a unilateral process but a genuine peace process. As I wrote already in 1975 the small-step method (Oslo in the past, and the road map today) is very debatable; it postpones all the fundamental problems and any incident or "road accident" can stop any progress.

In reality, between the Iraqi conflict and the future of Israeli-Palestinian relations, the links are weak, despite the conviction of the neoconservatives that a "satisfactory" settlement (i.e., a pro-Israeli one) of the Palestinian tragedy depends on the democratization of the Arab world, beginning with Iraq. It is an autonomous problem, even if, in the first Gulf War, victory was an opportunity to revive one more peace process. In the final analysis what will happen with this infernal cycle between Israelis and Palestinians will be broadly independent of the situation in Iraq.

The real choice, therefore, has to be between the exclusive priority given to the struggle against terrorism, a priority which obviously serves the cause of Israel—and the necessity, if one wants to reach a genuine settlement, of making Ariel Sharon and the Israelis understand that what matters is not just the end of terrorism but the evacuation of the occupied territories, including the settlements. This is what I have called, in an editorial that of course was not published by the *New York Times*, "It's the Occupation, Stupid!" We are very far from this. Sharon's attempt to prevent terrorist infiltration by the construction of a wall that encroaches on Palestinian territory is from this point of view a disaster. However, the strength of American Jewish organizations and of the so-called Christian right weighs in the direction of priority for anti-terrorist actions. Their program is very close to that of Likud. After his earlier meeting with Sharon and the new Palestinian prime minister, Bush received a letter signed by practically all the senators, which accused him of having been too pro-Palestinian, after which he repeated the objective of the total destruction of terrorism. The road map has been at the mercy of provocations, suicide bombings, and reprisals. As for the dream of the neoconservatives and of the Christian right, it is at best a very distant vision. Waiting for Syria, Iran, or Saudi Arabia to experience regime change is no solution. It would make them more pro-Palestinian and take a very long time. Moreover, the closer we approach the American election, the more both American parties, Democratic and Republican, will try to get the Jewish vote. From this point of view, there is an objective alliance between the terrorists of Hamas and the hard-line Israelis, supported by those American Jews who, like one of the Republican leaders in the House, Tom DeLay—who is not Jewish—wish for the failure of the road map.

One of the ideas originally endorsed by Bush and included in the road map was the establishment of a Palestinian state. But if one looks at realities on the ground, one sees that by now the possibility of such a state has been deeply compromised. Gaza evacuated by Israelis will be controlled by Hamas, and at its borders, by Egypt; the West Bank will be divided into at least two blocks of land that will have no border with each other and in which roads open only to the Israelis will continue to function. A large chunk of territory will be on the Israeli side of Sharon's wall.

Bozo: Let us move on to the postwar landscape in the United States. You have insisted on the national union that appeared after September 11 and made the Iraqi episode possible but today one sees much more clearly that the case for war in Iraq was a very weak one, concerning both the weapons of mass destruction and the links with al Qaeda. Can Bush keep his internal support as strong as before?

Hoffmann: Let's begin with the mystery of the weapons of mass destruction. Only two points are well established. All the intelligence agencies believed in them. And those weapons have been neither used nor found. Where did these agencies get their information? From dubious informants? From exiles eager to provoke the fall of Saddam? This has certainly been the case in Washington and in London. Moreover, if they had serious information, what then happened to the weapons? One knows, thanks to Mohammed Al Baradi's inspections, that Iraq had no real atomic program. One also knows that the inspections of 1991 to 1998 destroyed most of the stocks of biological and chemical weapons. What did Saddam do with those weapons that remained after such inspections? Why had he until the end given the impression that he had things to hide? Did he believe, as Hans Blix and David Kaye think, that this would deter his adversaries—abroad and at home—and preserve an already much reduced prestige, whereas in fact his maneuvers and his bad faith encouraged them to get rid of him? Did he succeed in exporting his stocks at the last minute? In any case, his military seem to have received no order to use any. Some of those questions are still unanswered, but let us remember the first Gulf War. It is not the first time that Saddam's behavior has had a suicidal aspect. The other mystery is that of the cases prepared in Washington and London in order to persuade public opinion of the seriousness of the Iraqi threat. Not only did they not persuade everybody, for instance traditional realists who knew that Iraq was not comparable to the former Soviet Union and that deterrence had a good chance of succeeding in the long run, or even experienced men like Brzezinski; but these prepared cases, by their very exaggeration, subsequently led to a political reaction. The debate has centered on the question of who lied to whom. Did the political leaders insist that the intelligence agencies present only firm conclusions and eliminate all doubts or skeptical formulations, or have those agencies themselves, knowing what their bosses wanted, initiated hyperboles? In Great Britain, where lying to Parliament is unforgivable, Tony Blair despite his majority in the House of Commons has heavily paid, in popularity and authority, for his fevered exaggerations (Iraqi arms are capable of striking in forty-five minutes). Even in the United States, many minds have been shaken but at first neither Congress nor the press showed much curiosity, so that public opinion appeared not to have been turned around by all this noise: the excuses presented by George Tenet, when he was the CIA's boss, and by Stephen Hadley, Condoleezza Rice's aide, on a minor point of Bush's State of the Union speech of January 2003, have made it possible for the president to continue to say that he had received excellent information and that his confidence in the intelligence agencies was undiminished. In any case, no parliamentary investigation has yet come to embarrass him directly unlike the inquiry into September 11. For the majority of public opinion, the elimination of the evil Saddam was more important than the nature of the arguments.

Bozo: One can however ask oneself about the length of support for the president. Before and during the war, political debate was pretty much suspended, if only because the opponents of the war—mainly from the Democratic side—were not able or did not want to take the political risk of breaking national unity, except perhaps for someone like Al Gore, who remained an isolated case. But this has changed very quickly: the postwar difficulties, the unsuccessful search for weapons of mass destruction, the problem of the truth or falsity of the presentation of the case by the administration before the war, doesn't all this change the situation? A few months away from the presidential election, can't one expect a real national debate, both on the past—Iraq—and on the future—what are the threats and what is the strategy to be used?

Hoffmann: In the beginning the Democrats appeared to want to concentrate on domestic politics only, because Bush and his team were rather vulnerable in this domain, the economy not being as robust as certain people had hoped. Remember that in the U.S. 41 million people have no health insurance and those who have it are threatened by the transfer of many social expenditures to the states which are obliged to balance their budgets and whose inhabitants often refuse to raise taxes. The contest would be very lively if people realized that the public services on which they depend every day in order to keep the roads clear in winter are defective, that decent public transportation has become problematic, and even that some schools have to close earlier every year because they have no money for their last weeks of classes. The percentage of poor people in the population has increased. Here, the Democrats have a good battlefield, but it may not be good enough. The economy has improved in 2004, productivity has increased, there has even been a rise in the number of jobs offered. Moreover, the Democrats will have to mobilize people who until now have been sufficiently discouraged to stay away from the voting booth. It is true that the difficulties in Iraq will allow the Democrats, if they are not too divided or too scared, to criticize foreign policy also.

The damage caused by unilateralism has become obvious, and so are the signs of division and disarray in the administration. There is no question of a quick return of the boys from Iraq. The threats on America's presence in Iraq and the political and military failure which is still looming in Afghanistan provoke for the time being no strong calls for disengagement but rather proposals for a massive increase of reconstruction tasks at a time when the budget deficit provoked by Bush's financial policies has risen. Hence the temptation of obtaining contributions from other countries, but why would they do so? Democrats will need to fully recover from their own foreign policy disarray. They have been rather cowardly except for the noncandidate Al Gore and the former candidate Howard Dean who appeared, to many, to be too wild in his criticisms. Even Hillary Clinton has given the example of someone who wants to avoid taking risks, although she is not an official candidate. At the time of the debate on the president's war powers, and of the vote by the two Houses in October 2002, she followed Bush without any hesitation.

Bozo: Beyond politics, all this raises the question of American society itself. One could have the feeling that September 11 transformed it to such an extent that, even though it remains a liberal democracy, it is less so than before and less than Europe. You have mentioned some of these aspects in chapter 3: a kind of state of emergency which reminds one of the twentieth-century wars, the acceptance by the citizens of certain restrictions on public liberties, a stifling, if not censorship, of debate; hasn't a return to normalcy now followed? Aren't we coming back to a more familiar America, thanks to events in Iraq and to the election campaign of 2004?

Hoffmann: It's true, the Democratic candidates are beginning to sound more vigorous, if only because the role of the missionary-sheriff is no longer so attractive. Debate has begun again over foreign policy—I hope one sees this in Europe—and this is good. But insofar as liberties are concerned, the Democrats have until now mainly criticized the government for not being energetic enough in maintaining security. Except for Howard Dean, little has been said by them on this subject. Restrictions on civil liberties and the policy of furtive dismantlement of social protections occur in such a way that many Americans don't even remark on it. In this regard, normalcy is still far away. Casualties and expenditures in Iraq force people to ask questions about the world role of the United States, but the domestic measures presented by officialdom as aimed at ensuring the security of the citizens reassure them more than they worry them. It will be interesting to see when this will stop being the case.

7

THE TRAP

(October 2003–August 2004)

As of now—August 2004—Iraq is still occupied, security has not been restored, many public services remain battered, and the re-creation of a legitimate political process is still in limbo. The worst is not always sure, but Iraq has so far been both an embarrassment and a trap for the Bush administration. It is an embarrassment because the most widely used arguments for the invasion—Saddam's weapons of mass destruction and his collusion with al Qaeda—have been proven false (we are still waiting for the congressional investigation of the intelligence provided to the U.S. government to tell us whether or not misinformation was partly the result of the administration's own pressure on the intelligence agencies, and it appears obvious that terrorism has received a boost from the invasion). Iraq is also a trap; it appears more and more like a huge kick into a poisoned ant hill, and all the options seem grim.

I.

It is certain that Iraq is not Vietnam—a moderately "happy end" is not totally ruled out—but we find once again very familiar flaws: wrong assumptions, immoderate and confused ends, served by a mixture of counterproductive, inadequate, mismanaged and, at times, scandalous means. I have discussed the assumptions in previous chapters. As for the ends, both Bush and Blair have had to go through quaint contortions in order to argue that Saddam's regime did indeed represent a major security threat for the U.S. and the world, or could have become one again—the former argument being hard to believe, and the latter one stretching the case for preventive war way beyond credibility. They have therefore insisted more and more on what I would call a double humanitarian argument: the liberation of the Iraqis from a horrible tyranny, and the goal of a democratic and moderate Iraq. The removal of the tyrant has been addressed before—an undeniable blessing surrounded by a mass of highly debatable legal justifications, and accomplished in a way that has, so far, left many Iraqis resentful. The goal of a democratic Iraq is even more controversial. Instant, or quasi-instant, democracy, in a country marked by so many cleavages (ethnic, religious, social—modern classes versus traditional status groups[1]), diverse solidarities or political ideologies, "a conflictual space in which secularism competes with Islamism, centralism with federalism, traditional patriarchy with the emancipation of women, and liberalism with statism"—and no experience of democracy. For the U.S. to create, or assist, in the creation of the institutions and the practices democracy requires would mean a very long occupation, and the need to fight a pro-

1. See Faleh A. Jabar, *Postconflict Iraq* (U.S. Institute of Peace, Special Report #120, May 2004).

tracted and motivated insurgency: this was not what the U.S. faced in Germany and Japan in 1945. Moreover, ignorance of Iraq's past, of its culture and history, is widespread among American elites and forces (one of the many merits of *Fahrenheit 9/11* is to show the clash of cultures between the young American soldiers and the traumatized Iraqis).

Democracy does not come fast, nor does it come from the outside. The outsider breeds nationalism against him. As J. G. Herder wrote more than two centuries ago, "the happiness of one people cannot be imposed upon any other. . . . The roses for the wreath of liberty must be picked by one's own hand, and they must have grown up joyfully out of their own needs, out of their own desires and love. . . . The yoke of an alien, badly introduced freedom would be a terrible nuisance for a foreign people."[2] Before a democratic Iraq can develop, there is a need for a genuine civil society and for basic institutions at the local level—as well as an impartial judiciary and a responsible bureaucracy. In other words, it must come out of state-building, and this can best be helped by the U.N., by the international community, not by the U.S. alone.

But is a democratic Iraq really the objective of the Bush administration? The rather pitiful sums devoted, in the U.S. budget, to nation-building in Afghanistan, and the lagging disbursement of funds for the recovery of Iraq, make one wonder. After all, a democratic Iraq may not support many of America's policies, especially in the Middle East. Majority rule may benefit Islamic Shi'ism, a formula aimed at protecting minorities may be resented and opposed by the Shi'ite majority. Isn't America's real objective a "friendly" Iraq? This is the best explanation for what has been called an attempt

---

2. See Ioannis D. Evrigenis and Daniel Pellerin, *Johann Gottfried Herder—Another Philosophy of History* (Cambridge, Mass.: Hackett Publishing Company, 2004), part V.

"not only to repair and selectively reform Iraq, but to virtually reinvent it—economically, socially, politically," thus displaying "a vision in which reform is conflated with foreign hegemony."[3] The prominent role given by the occupiers to Iraqi exiles with little support in the country but strong connections with the American intelligence services that financed them, the attribution of profitable contracts to American companies (such as, of course, Halliburton), the plans for the establishment of U.S. military bases, the very size of the new American embassy and its branches in the country, all this goes far beyond a mere concern for preventing the reemergence of a dangerous Iraq. It also goes a long way toward explaining the shift among Iraqis from happiness at being relieved of Saddam's tyranny to disenchantment with, and hostility to, the occupation.

The confusion and proliferation of objectives result from what I consider the original sin of the whole operation—as it was of the Vietnam War: ignorance of the local conditions, hubris about what the U.S. can hope to accomplish, unawareness of "the foreignness of foreigners,"[4] and neglect of Auguste Comte's warning: the nineteenth-century sociologist, contemporary of (but philosophically far away from) Tocqueville famously wrote that "one only destroys what one replaces," and the U.S. had no clear or effective design for replacement.

If we turn to the means, we can distinguish between mistakes and abuses. Some of the former were mentioned in chapter 6. The vagaries in the search for a political course continued: Paul Bremer's earlier decision to dissolve the

---

3. *Radical Departure: Toward a Practical Peace in Iraq*, Carl Conetta, Project on Defense Alternatives Briefing Report #16, July 8, 2004, at the Commonwealth Institute, Cambridge, Massachusetts.

4. I used this expression in *Gulliver's Troubles* (New York: McGraw Hill, 1968).

Ba'athist army and bureaucracy had thus fueled the resentment of the hundreds of thousands of Iraqis now unemployed. It left a void both for security and for reconstruction. He ended up moving back from his policy of total deba'athification, less because it had produced hundreds of thousands of foes of the occupation than because of the need to reconstitute security forces against the insurgents, and to reinstate technicians for the repair of basic services. Then, Washington decided on the transfer of (some) sovereignty to a new interim government—something Mr. Bremer had not appeared to favor. It was provided with a temporary constitution that proved to be a bone of contention between Shi'ites and Kurds, the former making it clear that the privileged position of the latter would not be accepted permanently. But even though the administration had appeared finally to turn to the U.N. for the selection of the members of the new government, and even though the U.N. representative had expressed his intention to select technocrats (probably so as not to prejudge the results of the elections scheduled for the end of 2004), the U.S. interfered in the process, insisted on the inclusion of political figures, and chose as head of the interim government a man who was not the U.N. candidate but a former employee of the CIA. This almost guaranteed a lack of legitimacy of the new "rulers" in the eyes of suspicious Iraqis. Moreover, the transfer of power was bound to remain limited, as the U.S. insisted on retaining control of military operations (with the interim government being, at most, consulted).

The vagaries in attitudes toward an insurgency that remains both intense and mysterious were also noticeable. Declarations of war on the rebels of Fallujah, in the Sunni triangle, and on the young Shi'ite cleric Al Sadr were followed by prudent retreats, as the attempts at killing or capturing the enemy would have been devastating for the civilian population. The U.S. encouraged the Iraqi authorities to recruit and train abundant security forces, but the many private militias remain in place, despite calls for their dissolution.

The whole occupation has been marked by an overestimation of Iraq's capacity for fast reconstruction and a quick return to security, and an underestimation of the funds needed and of the strength of internal antagonisms. Given the time needed to train Iraqi security forces, and the reluctance of their members to confront Iraqi rebels on behalf of the occupiers, it became obvious that the less than 140,000 coalition troops were simply too meager a contingent. But given Rumsfeld's determination to keep the numbers down (while saying that if the military asked for more he would give them what they wanted—but also making it clear that he was not encouraging them to ask!), the military had to resort to a variety of measures to prolong the stay of American troops beyond the time they had contracted for, thus increasing the unpopularity of the war with many families at home, and the proportion of men and women drawn from the National Guard and Reserves is now around 40 percent. If, as Michael Ignatieff has written, nation-building in Afghanistan was "nation-building lite," the occupation has been a military presence not exactly cheap (since new funds have become necessary) but meager—thus putting on the current interim government a burden it is not well equipped or legitimate enough to handle well.

Another feature of the occupation has been a high degree of confusion in the chain of command. It was not always evident that Mr. Bremer had full final authority over the military. It was not always evident that the commander of the coalition forces exerted full control over his subordinates, over the military police and, above all, over the intelligence bodies (when senators, especially Senator McCain, asked the Secretary of Defense to explain the chain of command, he turned to the military with whom he had come to the Senate, and they did not exactly provide him with an answer). Interservice rivalries did not end. The Marine commanders often boasted of having a better understanding of Iraqi concerns than the Army. The feud between the Pentagon and its intelligence suppliers on the one hand, and the CIA on the other, exploded in the spectacular raid of Iraqi forces escorted by CIA agents against Mr. Chalabi, the Pentagon's candidate for leadership, in May 2004, when the CIA argued that the controversial Chalabi had provided important information to Iran (not to mention the misinformation he had so abundantly provided to the U.S.).[5] The new head of the interim government, Mr. Allawi, was the CIA's man. Chalabi had received more than $300,000 a month until April, and the Pentagon's unhappiness at his demise was forcefully expressed by Richard Perle.

Much of all this has resembled the contortions of a foot caught in a mousetrap. Much of it was just the consequence of the initial unpreparedness and ignorance, some of it was a rather startling display of incompetence—startling because of the discipline the administration had observed in its stealthy march to war and during the brief war against Saddam. This incompetence extended to a kind of blindness toward bad symbolism: after the looting of the museums and hospitals came George W. Bush's promise to build a new central prison for the new sovereign Iraq, and of course the Abu Ghraib affair—in Saddam's former house of torture.

This brings us to abuses. Many have occurred at home. Some were finally dealt with by the Supreme Court (which,

---

5. See Jane Mayer, "The Manipulator," *The New Yorker*, June 7, 2004, pp. 58–72; and Thomas Powers, in Mark Follman, "A Temporary Coup," Salon.com: http://archive.salon.com/news/feature/2004/06/14/coup/index_np.html. If Chalabi did indeed serve Iranian interests, the Iranians will have brilliantly succeeded in a double whammy: they have gotten the Americans to get rid of their enemy Saddam Hussein and to remain stuck in Iraq, which deters any likely attack on Iran.

however, left standing the bizarre category of "enemy combatants"). Many provisions of the Patriot Act remain to be tested in courts. One of the most extraordinary is the attempt by Pentagon-serving lawyers to argue that the president's "commander-in-chief authority" allows him to do all that is required for the protection of the U.S.—including authorizing torture (the administration had already decided not to apply the Geneva Conventions to prisoners in Afghanistan, nor to enforce the Conventions against torture and other cruel, inhuman, and degrading treatment or punishment).[6]

This was, of course, the background to the cruel, inhuman, and degrading practices that were used at Abu Ghraib. From the Red Cross protests of 2002 to the revelations of the spring of 2004, there is enough evidence to show that these horrid treatments were not just the acts of a few "rotten apples" in a barrel, but, as one psychologist put it, the product of the barrel itself, nor were they limited to one prison. It is clear that at Abu Ghraib military intelligence officers had pushed aside the prison's commander, and that the high command either did not read reports that described violations, or failed to intervene forcefully in the places where they were committed. That the investigations ordered by the army resulted in a whitewash was not surprising (self-investigation is not exactly a guarantee of justice). So far, only low-level soldiers and guards have been indicted or condemned—a fact that has only strengthened the catastrophic effect the pictures from Abu Ghraib have had, not only in the Muslim world, but everywhere.

Other abuses are the almost inevitable results of counterinsurgency actions by forces that are not equipped, materially or

---

6. See the *Working Group Report on Detainee Interrogations in the Global War on Terrorism* (March 6, 2003), and Anthony Lewis, "Making Torture Legal," *New York Review of Books*, July 15, 2004, pp. 4–8.

psychologically, for a kind of warfare that aims at avoiding or minimizing "collateral damage." From brutal intrusions into suspects' homes to air strikes that kill indiscriminately innocent civilians and suspects, such actions have done a great deal to foster either outright hostility or a modicum of support for the insurgents (as long as they themselves do not kill Iraqis indiscriminately). This problem is one of many that illustrate the American dilemma in Iraq: moderation in the form of some tacit accommodation with insurgents and resisters leaves them in at least partial control, all-out assaults on them play into their hands, insofar as popular support is concerned. Both approaches have been tried in Fallujah and Najaf.

A last form of abuse is a practice that is beginning to attract attention—the "outsourcing," or privatization, of war-related activities. The problem with entrusting what used to be public responsibilities to private, profit-seeking entrepreneurs is partly (but only partly) caused by the need to keep the size of U.S. forces down. It results in a high degree of irresponsibility: the employees of these private operations are answerable only to their bosses, not to the military or to the public bureaucrats who employ them. This has been one factor in the Abu Ghraib debacle. In the 1990s, the CIA "outsourced the Iraq project"—aimed at "creating the conditions for the removal of Saddam Hussein from power," as instructed by the first President Bush—to a firm specializing in "perception management," the Rendon Group, which "was charged with the delicate task of helping to create a viable and united opposition movement against Saddam," and used Chalabi for this purpose (he had CIA support until 1996).[7] One of the most striking aspects of the administration's attitude toward its mistakes and abuses has been the apparent immunity of all those responsible (and the 9/11 Commission, determined to present

7. Jane Mayer, op. cit., pp. 61–62.

a unanimous report, has preferred spreading blame to specifying it). Nobody has resigned except Tenet, nobody has been fired.

II.

What is to be done? There are many who believe that the U.S. has to "stay the course," and that—especially after having failed to support various insurrections against Saddam, in 1991 after the Gulf War, in Kurdistan in 1996—American credibility is at stake. Moreover, especially on the Republican side, the mix of the mirage of democracy for Iraq and the whole region, and the desire for a reliable Iraq, is a potent argument for helping not only the interim government, but the one that would emerge from the forthcoming election, to defeat the insurgencies. The spread of terrorism in Iraq makes it difficult to sort out Islamist terrorists from outside the country, or Iraqi postwar affiliates of bin Laden, from Iraqi insurgents against the occupation; thus, the war against terrorism that has become an American priority and obsession ends by achieving the very amalgamation between Iraq and al Qaeda that the administration had falsely denounced. Others point out that the prolonged occupation "is an open invitation for a steady buildup of grassroots Muslim anger,"[8] and a breeding ground for terrorism in a country where, under Saddam, terror was strictly aimed at Iraqis disloyal to him.

At present, much of the insurgency is aimed, not principally at the American occupiers, but at oil pipelines and at deterring other members of the coalition, private entrepreneurs from abroad, and ordinary technicians and Iraqis, from working for

---

8. Christopher Preble (director), *Exiting Iraq*. Report of a special task force sponsored by the Cato Institute (Washington, D.C.: 2004), p. 30.

and with the Americans. It may well be that many Iraqis currently disgruntled with the occupation will be increasingly revolted by the killings of Iraqis by the insurgents and by the insecurity they foster. In this case, an Iraqi policy of repression may become popular or at least accepted. But as long as it will need the muscular support of American forces, it also risks being caught in the trap. Those who, especially among the Democrats, call on NATO or on other foreign forces to join the American and British ones and thus to help stabilize Iraq and its new institutions need to realize that this is less a solution—even if such forces receive a U.N. mandate—than wishful thinking. Those NATO countries that favored the "coalition" are already (or—in Spain's case—were) in it. France and Germany are very unlikely to join; the French concern with not giving to the Muslim world the image of "the West versus Islam" will not vanish. As for Muslim countries, their enthusiasm for moving to help Iraqi authorities as long as the "coalition" is still in military control is not visible. Others may come in, either to help train Iraqi forces, or to join them, only if the Americans leave.

There are good reasons for calling for the end of the occupation. As in Palestine, the occupation is the main cause of the current troubles (which does not mean that they will end if we leave; but whatever we do to try to resolve the internal conflicts is likely to backfire). Continuing U.S. military control, direct or indirect, will feed anti-Americanism (as in post-1965 South Vietnam) and provide a training and breeding ground for terrorism, native and from other countries. American interests would be better served by a shift of U.S. resources toward, on the one hand, the fight against al Qaeda and its allies around the world—who have become more diversified and decentralized and continue to receive manpower and support from schools and factions in officially pro-American states such as Saudi Arabia and Pakistan—and, on the other hand, toward a much more massive program aimed at rebuilding the economic infrastructure of Iraq and at helping establish new institutions with the help of other states experienced in state-building. The exit of American and British forces would make it easier for countries that have not supported the war to provide assistance (including police training) under U.N. auspices. Those who argue that "a permanent (U.S.) military garrison in Iraq" would "impose enormous costs and a host of new headaches for the American taxpayers and the military alike," and that the American military presence in Iraq contributes "to a worsening perception of the United States by a growing number of Muslims" (and, I would add, non-Muslims) are right.[9] It is time to refocus the struggle against terrorism, by giving priority to the fight against Islamic jihadists (the most dangerous for U.S. and Western interests), and by spending far more energy on a permanent solution to the Palestinian problem, along the lines almost agreed upon at Taba in 2001 and advocated by the Geneva informal alliance of Palestinians and Israelis, as well as by Jimmy Carter.

What would such an exit strategy mean, concretely? It would require a statement by the coalition of its intention to withdraw its forces by a certain date: let us say, within six months of the establishment of a newly elected assembly and government that emanates from it, and no later than the end of June 2005. During the period of the present interim government, the U.S. would take measures endowed with genuine political and symbolic significance: a "normalization" of the size and nature of the U.S. Embassy, the elimination of formal U.S. advisors in the ministries, granting the Iraqi government the right to ask for military operations, a commitment not to launch any unless they are so requested, and the

9. Ibid., p. 17.

removal of the U.S. from the preparation and supervision of the coming elections—these should be left to the U.N., which could cancel or replace the decisions made about ballot access by commissions set up by Bremer (only the certifiable criminals of the Ba'ath army and bureaucracy ought to be kept out, as well as terrorists condemned for their actions). During this period, the training of Iraqi security forces might, of necessity, remain a coalition task, but it ought to be monitored and supervised by the U.N.

After the elections, the withdrawal of coalition forces would begin. They would be replaced by Iraqis and by the forces of any country—including the U.S. and the U.K.—that is acceptable by the Iraqis and accepts to participate in an international peace-making and peace-keeping force, constituted with the consent of the new Iraqi government and placed under the control of the U.N. The command would be Iraqi. The new government would have the right to renegotiate the contracts attributed by the coalition and to decide on a permanent status for the oil industry. No foreign bases would be established in Iraq.

Such a policy would be more of an embarrassment than an opportunity for anti-American insurgents and terrorists: they could no longer argue that Iraq is an American outpost with a government chosen by Washington. If they continue their fight, and if it can be shown that an increasingly large number among them are from outside Iraq, they would risk unifying Iraq's new political forces and peoples against them. Successful counterinsurgency requires popular support, and foreign occupation inhibits such support. Conversely, the longer the occupation remains in Iraq, the more difficult extrication will get. It is particularly important that the U.S. allows the Iraqis to decide on the nature of their future government, and on the substance of their new permanent constitution.

There is no doubt that the course advocated here entails

risks. A breakup of the country because of its multiple lines of fracture is by no means ruled out. It could lead to a civil war, or to foreign interventions, say, by Iran helping Iraqi Shi'ite clerics, or by Turkey trying to prevent Kurdish secession. These risks partly explained why the first Bush administration was so reluctant to intervene in the domestic affairs of Iraq, and to get caught in the turmoil. The prevention of a bloody disintegration of Iraq, the prevention of a takeover of Iraq by Islamic extremist terrorists in case new Iraqi security forces do not suffice, ought to be left to international diplomacy by the U.N. and regional organizations, as well as to international peace-making forces provided by them.

Would such an American policy be one of defeatism and weakness? On the one hand, remaining trapped among equally unsavory choices would weigh heavily on U.S. foreign policy in general (de Gaulle had understood this in the case of Algeria, and sugested this to the U.S., in vain, in that of Indochina). On the other hand, Americans will be able to argue that they helped Iraq decisively by eliminating Saddam (at a heavy cost in international support and prestige), that they gave Iraq back to its people, that it is now up to the Iraqis to make a success or a mess out of it with the help of the international community whenever it is needed, and that the best the U.S. can still do is not to fight the vicious circle of a counterinsurgency war, but to shift resources toward aid for reconstruction and development, as well as to take part in genuinely international peace-making and peace-keeping if the Iraqis call for American participation.

Nothing wholly good can come out of a war that resulted from a mix of self-deception and deliberate deception, waged in a part of the world in which alien control has for a long time fostered turmoil and tragedy. The presence of terrorism is not an invitation to empire, but an incentive for finding policies that reduce its appeal, and for pursuing the terrorists in ways that do not help them multiply. In the case of the Middle East, an exit from Iraq, combined with a new effort by the U.S., the U.N., the EU, and Russia to end the Israeli occupation of Palestinian lands and to create a livable Palestinian state, would mark a return to reality, to good sense, and to morality.

8

THE FUTURE OF THE INTERNATIONAL SYSTEM

Bozo: Let us talk about the future of the international order, if there is any. Let us begin with the question of the U.N. It was both the main stake in the Iraqi crisis and its victim. Today the problem of the U.N. determines many others, including that of alliances. Some of the present policymakers in America, namely the neoconservatives, don't conceal their desire to put an end to this U.N. system which they deem altogether useless, illegitimate, and even damaging because it constrains American power. Is an international order possible without the U.N.?

Hoffmann: If by United Nations, one means the members of the U.N., the Security Council, and the General Assembly, things will not change much, even if one talks about big reform projects. It is very difficult to reform this institution, since the permanent members of the Security Council have a right of veto on all eventual provisions. This actually reflects the state of international order, or disorder. However, one cannot do without the Assembly and the Security Council. When Americans attack the U.N. in general it is more the Secretary General, the bureaucracy, and the weight (especially in the Assembly) of countries which have no military power and are economically dependent. It is a debate which has gone on for a long time. The neoconservatives believed for a while that they had reached their goal; they even talked about replacing France on the Security Council with India, but the battle goes on. A large part of the media and the members of Congress now understand the symbolic and practical importance of the U.N.

This is not entirely new. During the cold war, the United Nations managed to survive and be active at least on secondary issues. During the 1950s and 1960s, the U.N. played an important role in the movement for decolonization, as a force for legitimation. Now that there are no more colonies, the U.N. is perceived by many countries as the guardian of the sovereignty of these new independent states, and as an institution capable of playing an important role of intervention in civil wars, as well as a role in peacekeeping—on the condition that the Americans wish for or permit it. This is not insignificant.

Bozo: During the Cold War, the Security Council had been paralyzed, and the U.N. relegated to dealing with secondary issues, but it was not so bad since in the last analysis international order rested on the balance between the two blocs. That balance having disappeared after 1989, the Security Council has tried as best it could to play a regulating role in the use of force, which actually is its domain, according to the charter. Thus the Council was until now protector of a certain international order which is currently totally challenged. Isn't this worrisome?

Hoffmann: Certainly. In a militarily unipolar world the dominant power has to be limited, contained, authorized, by an authority which may be debatable but widely accepted. The U.N. thus has an indispensable role. We are going back to an idea which was not taken sufficiently seriously because it was premature, the idea expressed by Dag Hammarskjöld, the Secretary General of the U.N. during the Congo crisis of 1960, that "we are here to protect the small ones." Americans had not been fond of this statement, and de Gaulle's France even less so. But it is certain that the protection of these countries must be assured. The Americans around Bush proclaim that they can very well be in charge of world order by themselves, and that others don't count, but they overestimate once more the power of the U.S., except for brute force, and above all its prestige, which has been deeply damaged.

Bozo: In the indictment of the U.N. and the Security Council by the neoconservatives, there is an attack on the nondemocratic character of the world organization, made up as it is of nondemocratic governments which, alas, is not exactly wrong. But isn't there in this indictment a confusion between the notion of democracy which is indeed rare in the U.N. system, and that of the rule of law, which is the real mission of the U.N. and of the Council?

Hoffmann: The answer that the neoconservatives would give you is this: "We Americans, because we insure the rule of law in the world, and are the guardians of world order, we are free to select in the enormous mass of treaties and norms those provisions which deserve to be kept and those which seem obsolete." This was already, two or three years ago, the meaning of the writings of a professor of law at Yale University, Michael Reisman, who thus gave, without being perhaps completely aware of it, the very definition of empire. Then, with the war in Iraq, this imperial temptation has gotten bigger among some lawyers, paradoxically happy to see that one has finally come back to "reality," i.e., an era in which the relations of might prevail over law. Their speech can be summed up as follows: "If it is on us that international order rests, let us not be hypocrites and let us recognize this fact, especially as we are the servants of liberty and democracy. Our imperialism is a benevolent one." (It must be said that this imperialism is not always particularly benevolent: think of the lawyers who advised the Pentagon about the legality of torture in Iraqi jails.) The more the world looks like a jungle, partly because of terrorism, the more it needs norms.

Bozo: Are there other ways, more acceptable to the rest of the world, of assuring the compatibility between democracy and the rule of law in international society, for instance, by democratizing the U.N.?

Hoffmann: There are two main problems here. The first is that the rule of pure force is a major regression, an invitation to transform an obviously imperfect order into a jungle in which a great power would decide what targets to hit, what regimes to punish, etc., and this would inevitably be imitated by others who have their own accounts to settle. In this world we need a force that is legitimate but contained (legitimate because it is contained), hence the rightness of the French position in the Iraqi crisis. The second problem is that of democracy and human rights. How should one handle states which mistreat or murder their own citizens? As I've said before, it is not a question the U.N. will be spontaneously capable of resolving because too many of its members have dirty regimes and their representatives will do all they can to block any proposal for collective military intervention aimed at regime change.

We need a system with two stages: first, a group of members of the U.N. would ask the Security Council to authorize a collective intervention to overthrow a regime responsible for unacceptable atrocities. Second, if the Security Council refuses or is incapable of acting, then appeals should be addressed to a new institution, an association of democratic nations, which would include the members of NATO, and the democracies of Asia, Africa, and Latin America, such as India, South Africa, Chile, as well as Australia and New Zealand. Only the liberal democracies, graced with representative governments which are respectful of human rights and practice the separation of powers, could be members of this association. If it approved a collective intervention to change a regime, it would explain its reasons and would give an account of its actions to the Secretary General of the U.N. Such an association of democratic nations could also give useful advice to new democracies (as the Council of Europe did to East European countries after Communism) and bring before the International Criminal Court or a special international criminal court the military or civilian leaders responsible for crimes against humanity, war crimes, or genocide. Alas, one cannot count on the Bush administration for such a reform!

There is a precedent, the grouping created a few years ago in Warsaw by Madeleine Albright, for the promotion of democracy. She writes about it in her memoirs. What I propose is somewhat different: this association of democratic nations would have to be open to those of the third world, and also meet precise and stringent criteria of democracy—free elections are not enough. What Fareed Zakaria has called "illiberal democracies" would not be invited into it. One would need states respectful of the separation of powers, the freedom of media, the independence of justice and human rights. It would not be a large crowd. Moreover, this association, unlike Mrs. Albright's, would not have the mission of proselytizing for democracy, but the mission of deciding whether such and such a tyrannical regime needs to be overthrown, if necessary by force, or if its leaders should be indicted before international criminal courts. It is not an attempt to replace the U.N., but an attempt to fill a gap in the big tapestry of the Charter.

Bozo: Even if one accepts the argument of the neoconservatives, according to whom America is the best arbiter of freedom, democracy, and security, can't one reject this point of view by pointing out the danger of this conception, which is that other states like Russia and China could perhaps also use this argument, which is, deep down, merely an apology of force, for less respectable ends? Could one deter such imitators? Could American might do it all by itself?

Hoffmann: This is indeed the problem. Anybody could use such a doctrine; anybody could say, "I have the right to do this or that." But the only way of preventing this is by coercion or threats. One thus goes back to the rule of force. The Americans realized during the Vietnam War that this conception did not always and everywhere work well and that, in the long run, one risked losing all sympathy from other nations and inciting others to become counterweights. From this viewpoint, it is the contempt of many people around George Bush for any instituted international organization that scares me most. It is absolutely necessary, even in the interest of the lone superpower, that there exist limits. Without them, it will commit huge mistakes at the expense not only of others but of its own interests. In foreign policy, self-limitation, the respect for norms, for international law and institutions, can increase the real might of a strong country even if these norms limit the most extreme uses of military power.

Bozo: Would one reason for this contempt be the ineffectiveness of U.N. institutions, for instance, in the matter of nuclear proliferation?

Hoffmann: Here too things are complex. The nuclear nonproliferation treaty needs to be reinforced. To do that, a new series of measures would be necessary: it should be made more difficult for states to renounce the treaty, more intrusive inspections should be allowed, they should be less liable to restrictions imposed by the states under inspection and, finally, a serious study of the sanctions that need to be taken if there are violations discovered by the inspectors would have to be undertaken; this would entail a commitment by the Security Council to act with determination when the inspectors ring the alarm. In any case, the choice for the international system is simple; either the United States will designate the "good" proliferators and punish the "bad" ones—this would be the rule both of force and of arbitrariness—or else one will have to resort to the U.N. The hesitations of Washington in the face of the cases of Iran and North Korea show that even within the Bush administration many have understood that the United States alone cannot solve that question.

Bozo: Let us talk now of the Atlantic Alliance, which has been very shaken up by the Iraq crisis. After having survived the end of the cold war, NATO had asserted itself in the 1990s as one of the pillars of international security, complementing indeed the U.N., especially in the Balkans. Let us not forget that the Atlantic Alliance, with some exceptions, linked together the richest and most powerful democratic countries of the world. However, its future appears uncertain. Is it mainly because its leader currently rejects the rules of the game of collective security, which it had defined itself, or because its allies are bad allies?

Hoffmann: For the neoconservatives and their friends, what happens in the world is a pure and simple game of power, and the main usefulness of an organization like NATO is to serve as a pond in which docile countries can be fished and counted on by the U.S. in case of a conflict. Thus, in the eyes of the Pentagon, the function of NATO is limited from now on to the use it can make of it. If the situation gets worse in the Near East or the Middle East, Europe is the area closest to those regions. The United States can put forces and build bases there. For this the alliance remains very useful, but it is mainly countries approved by the U.S. and not NATO as an organization (with the exception of the Afghan case, where the U.S. has called on NATO to replace American forces). This means that NATO is not considered as necessary for managing a common policy; indeed it could be a source of complications. This is very serious. The Atlantic Alliance has been, from Dean Acheson to Madeleine Albright, the holy arch of American foreign policy. Now it is in Romania and Bulgaria, countries that have only recently joined NATO, that American bases will be built.

Bozo: On the whole, the Americans tell the Europeans, "You do not represent any more the strategic problem that you were during the cold war and immediately after it. But you don't contribute either to the solution of our current strategic problems." In other words, Europe is no longer for us a security concern now that the Soviet threat has disappeared and that stability at the periphery of Europe, especially in the Balkans, is ensured. Therefore, the Europeans have to demonstrate their usefulness in supporting the U.S. in the rest of the world or else the alliance will fade. What can we answer?

Hoffmann: This reminds me of what the new president of my university told the members of the Divinity School, "One can take you seriously because of September 11, but does Harvard need a faculty of theologians?" The answer of one of them, one of the most eminent, was, "We mattered even in August!"

The neoconservatives consider that, from the point of view of democracy, the U.N. is a bunch of corrupt states; they are not entirely wrong. NATO is not, but this would not prevent people such as Richard Perle or Paul Wolfowitz from telling you bluntly that it is in the interest of the Europeans to stay in the Alliance because it protects them and that they therefore must obey, since the Americans glorify themselves in seeing farther than they do. Alas, things are not quite so simple. The "unexpected" pacifism of the Germans and the resistance of France are an obstacle to America's will prevailing in the alliance. In the case of France, Washington has forgotten a little quickly that the same Chirac who said "no" in January 2003 had been willing to reintegrate NATO in 1995 on condition that the U.S. redistribute the military commands, which the Pentagon refused to do, and they also forget that in Bosnia and Kosovo Chirac had been a dynamic and effective actor, if not a docile one.

Bozo: When one looks at the creation of NATO, one sees that it resulted from three constitutive elements: the perception of a common threat, which is no longer there, and which September 11 has not really replaced, at least for the Europeans; a common acceptance of the U.N.'s objectives and in particular of collective security, which the Americans seem to question; finally, the idea of a democratic community, of an alliance of liberal democracies. But can one preserve an alliance only because of common values?

Hoffmann: No, one also needs common interests and a common code of behavior and, if the allies are treated like tins of shoe polish for American boots, one isn't going to go very far. What dominates among the neoconservatives is the politics of contempt. This attitude, it must be said, is not particularly popular in the country: the American people are not fundamentally hypernationalist nor are they isolationist. But many are afraid; they like being among the strongest, because it is reassuring, and they certainly don't like that other countries tread on them. It is true that in public opinion polls one doesn't see any antimultilateralist movement but one has to notice that the popularity of the U.N. is low because Americans have been partly brainwashed. Deep down, I think that Americans, contrary to the present reading, accept the idea that if a conflict becomes acute or expensive, that if American soldiers are engaged in such a conflict and carry out tasks for which they are not ready, it should be possible to call on allies. The obstacle has been the Executive.

Bozo: Let us come now to the European Union. What balance sheet can one draw from the absence of Europe in the Iraqi affair? Let me formulate my question as follows: between Blair's approach, which aimed at influencing the United States so to speak from the inside, and Chirac's, which tries to influence by opposition, which one has succeeded best?

Hoffmann: Neither the frontal opposition of France nor the politics of solidarity of Blair have succeeded. It is indeed for that reason that one should begin by reconnecting France and Britain. Of course many of the American neoconservatives will argue that in any case, in the diplomatic and strategic domain, as Raymond Aron called it, Europe has no chance at counting, whether it is united or divided into twenty-five countries. This is, in essence, the thesis of Robert Kagan. It doesn't strike me as quite accurate. Already, as William Wallace has pointed out, "some 60,000–70,000 European troops have been sustained on operations outside the EU throughout 2003"—from the Balkans to Kabul. The European military effort, despite the ironic glance of the United States, will end up by having a certain impact. The cartoonish image of the Europeans in this domain, which is spread by the media, and especially Fox News on television, will no longer be able to prevail. The Europeans will be able to offer whatever forces they have in order to defend the security of other countries, including in Eastern Europe and maybe also in Asia, as long as it isn't from the Apocalypse that they have to be protected. On the contrary, if the Europeans do nothing and follow the advice of those who tell them, "Let us not waste our money on military expenditures, and let us not try to be a real power," they will not be able to play much of a role in international affairs.

Bozo: But isn't there once again a problem of presentation of French policy? Can one hope to progress on the road to a European defense if one talks about becoming a countervailing force or a balancing force vis-à-vis the United States or if one talks about a multipolar world? Even if nobody seriously imagines that Europe could compete with the United States in the strategic domain, wouldn't such rhetoric be capable of sinking the whole project in advance?

Hoffmann: It is certainly not the best way of presenting things even if, deep down, that is indeed what is at stake: finding a way of weighing on America's positions or of influencing them. But you are right, one should not talk in such terms. Americans have always been allergic to the classical balancing policies that Wilson had denounced. As for the neorealists of Kenneth Waltz's school, they prefer, in the name of stability, a unipolar or bipolar world to a multipolar one. However, even if one recognizes that the United States is most likely to remain a superpower for a very long time, one is entitled to think that other countries or organized regions will be able to play a considerable role.

Bozo: Isn't it necessary to state, modestly, that Europe's ambition is to assure stability on its borders—first of all, in the Balkans—and perhaps, in time, the security and defense of the Union itself? This objective would be unopposable by the United States, who might see in it in addition the promise of a Europe capable of assuming a burden that still weighs on the U.S, that of Europe's security. It would be, at the same time, a way for the Union to emancipate itself: the less Europe would depend on America for its own security, the more it will be free to make strategic choices beyond the old continent and the more the partnership with the United States—which is obviously necessary—would be balanced.

Hoffmann: Yes, as long as one is prudent in presenting such a policy. If one says: "We understand that despite your power, you cannot do everything yourselves and, besides, your resources are not inexhaustible; there are areas of the world that we know better than you do and where your lack of popularity doesn't allow you to get everyone to follow you," then the average American will probably not disagree. But above all one should not mention the good old policy of counterbalance. One therefore has to adopt the familiar rhetoric of interests: an absolutely dominant power often needs help. It is not in that power's interests to see the world only from the angle of its own force; it needs to be able to lean on an Antigone who could know how to lead Oedipus away from the precipice.

Hoffmann: Indeed. I have been quite struck by Greece's transformation; it has become a real European country where the people think like Europeans and even have nice things to say about Turkey; they have liberated themselves, to a large extent, of the weight of their own history by becoming good European students, relatively prosperous—which had not been the case before—and for whom the future is certainly Europe, not a neutral Europe, because the Greeks are not neutralists. One notices the same phenomenon in the other countries of the Union. The Americans do not know it sufficiently and still see in Europe a sort of hedonists' paradise; there too, Robert Kagan, in opposing a Venus-like Europe to a martial America, draws a cartoon. The Americans need to understand what is happening in Europe. It is true that it's taken time for Europe to construct itself but, from the point of view of history, fifty years are not much, when one thinks of the fratricidal hatreds that tore it apart in the past. Thus, to consider the Europe of today as if it were still the Europe of the 1930s—including the antisemitism of those days—means not understanding its evolution. What the bureaucratic machinery of the European Union lacks perhaps most is an good Minister of Communications. Power is so dispersed and complicated, with its multiple majority rules only a lawyer can understand, that it's difficult to explain it abroad. Commentaries in the American media about the constitutional document produced by the Convention have almost all adopted a tone of commiseration: "These Europeans are still at the stage of an ineffective confederation which, in America, only lasted a few years!" The Americans still haven't understood that the old European nations have very little in common with the English colonies that revolted against London, and that if the Europe of states is still stumbling, a Europe of minds, of interests, and of the young is taking shape, at the ground level.

Bozo: There is another encouraging element: many people have compared the current European crisis and that of the 1960s when the "European" Europe of de Gaulle was opposed to the "Atlantic" Europe of France's partners. But there is a great difference today: in those years the Atlanticists were federalists, and the partisans of an autonomous Europe were for an intergovernmental set-up which had an inhibiting effect on the political capacity of assertion of Europe. Today, those who advocate a powerful Europe, the "old Europe," according to Donald Rumsfeld, also are the most favorable to a transformation in a more federal direction; even the French are moving in this way, if one looks at the work of the Convention, whereas the defenders of sovereignty, Great Britain and the so-called new Europe are Atlanticists.

Hoffmann: You are quite right. It is an important reversal and I'm afraid that the British, indeed, have not yet reached that stage. But they are intelligent, pragmatic and likely to understand at the end that they have to evolve. It is quite possible that this Iraqi affair will have been the last manifestation of the "special relationship" with the U.S. Already the decision of Tony Blair to turn Britain toward Europe at the summit of St. Malo in 1998 was quite surprising. If he had done so it was because he understood that for the U.S. Europe was no longer the main concern.

Bozo: Let us end our discussions by coming back to the case of France. After the great theater of de Gaulle, hasn't the moment arrived for a more modest policy?

Hoffmann: De Gaulle himself knew how to adapt. Sometimes he did the opposite of what he had said while pretending that it was the same thing. In this case I don't think he would have failed to assert, even noisily, great principles; however, he would certainly have disapproved of any policy that would consist in asserting that we have to follow the Americans since we have lost our power. It must be said in this respect that there is a Vichy virus in a part of the French elite which is quite obnoxious. As far as Europe is concerned, progress is obvious. Fifteen or twenty years ago, much of the French bureaucratic personnel, and particularly the French diplomatic personnel, were very reluctant about any transfer of sovereignty. This is not the case today. The transformation of the curriculum of Sciences Po—my old school—and of the Ecole nationale d'administration show that there is a desire to be open to the world. Young French diplomats are often more pragmatic and less dogmatic than the Americans.

Bozo: So we end on a relatively optimistic note.

Hoffmann: Let's not be in a hurry! For many officials and members of Washington think tanks, especially among the neoconservatives, the European Union, supported by all previous administrations, sometimes as under Kissinger with a little bit of skepticism, is considered as a potential source of trouble. As for the "new Europe" dear to Rumsfeld, will it remain an American Trojan horse once its members are caught in the net of Brussels institutions? With its single currency and despite the slowdown of growth, with its capacity to attract and to export, the Union is the most serious competitor of the United States. But its military efforts are considered to be superfluous by Washington, which asks: why should we not leave these "martial" tasks to America? Some even ask if American wouldn't have an interest in keeping Europeans divided, in slowing down integration, or even in "disaggregating" the Union. If the reforms outlined in the draft constitution prepared by Valéry Giscard d'Estaing are adopted nothing will be more important to the Union than an excellent foreign minister selected for his talent rather than for his nationality. Next to an overbearing and unpopular America, Europe should have an important role: reassuring and helping the weak while trying to have a moderating impact on the United States.[1]

1. See the excellent indictment by Clyde Prestowitz in his book *Rogue Nation* (New York: Basic Books, 2003) and also, for the period of the younger Bush, the hard-hitting book of John Newhouse, *Imperial America* (New York: Knopf, 2003).

CONCLUSION

The Dangers of Empire

In August 2004 one can only establish a temporary balance sheet of the American adventure in Iraq. The recent troubles of the occupation, the continuation of violence and insecurity, the indignation evoked by the revelations about the Abu Ghraib jail, all of this has provoked in Washington a sharp and bitter debate on what should be done to put an end to the disaster and despite the United Nations resolution approving the transfer of power on July 1, 2004, to an interim Iraqi government, nobody yet knows how the drama will end. But one can already draw three major conclusions from this affair, which has dominated international relations for the last three years. The first concerns Iraq, the second the crisis of international order, and the third American society. Iraq has become a trap for the Americans and a godsend for the terrorists. International order has been badly affected by the paradoxically convergent blows of the Americans and the terrorists. The United States has gone through a phase of authoritarian and reactionary regression which is full of dangers.

The first conclusion concerns the war in Iraq. We know how the story began. The war has been a voluntary one, decided by a coalition of neoconservatives and other leaders eager for revenge. They have exploited the events of September 11, the anguish of a nation shocked by the brutal revelation of its new insecurity, the rise of a wounded patriotism and of a collective will to prove to the enemy and to the whole world the unlimited American capacity for reaction. Hence two effects: first, unanimity for the war in Afghanistan, then the relative ease with which Americans followed the lead of those who insisted on the need to drive Saddam Hussein from power, on the threat of his weapons of mass destruction for the security of his neighbors and of the United States, and on the presumed collusion between a state armed with terror weapons and the terrorism of al Qaeda. Thus, accounts would be settled with a tyrant whom one had failed to strike down at the end of the first Gulf War. The brief war of March-April 2003 revealed the extreme military weakness of the Iraqi regime and threw doubt on everything that had been said to magnify the threat it represented. Weapons of mass destruction were neither used nor found.

Victory has led to the occupation of an Arab country which was both fragmented and nationalist by a superpower which is militarily invincible and endowed with unprecedented technological advantages, but whose expectations were almost totally inadequate and whose ideas were mainly wrong for the preparation of the postwar period. This was due to several factors. There was the conviction that the occupying coalition would be greeted by the Iraqis with gratitude and relief, that the non-Ba'athist elements of Saddam's army and other Ba'athists who were close to or at the service of the exiles would come over to the Americans, ensure security, and thus make possible the rapid rebirth of democratic institutions in a country that had never had any. There was the very dubious hypothesis that these democratic institutions—in a country with a strong nationalism—would put themselves at the service of the great idea of the neoconservative reign: use Iraq as a lever to transform the Arab world and replace hostile regimes and dubious allies with governments that would be more democratic, more moderate, better disposed to make concessions to Israel. There was also the nature of the American army, an army for quick conquest, very eager to limit its losses and hence its risks, admirably ready and equipped for battle, but neither prepared nor gifted nor well disposed for police operations (unlike many other armies used by the U.N. to preserve peace in ethnic conflicts); moreover, this volunteer army was deliberately kept small by the Secretary of Defense despite the open or more concealed misgivings of the military leaders. Finally, there was a profound contradiction in the foreign policy of George W. Bush, between an imperial vision of America's role in the universal war against terrorism, in which deterrence would be replaced by preventive war, and profound distrust toward nation-building, considered both as an unworthy goal for American might and as a trap. This has been quite visible in Afghanistan and in Liberia.

After sixteen months of occupation, the preparation of Iraq for self-government has finally made some progress. But not enough: the Governing Council appointed by the United States, where former exiles dominated, has been dismissed but the new interim government which the U.N. was going to designate was still largely appointed by the U.S. and hence has a deficit of credibility and authority: insecurity in the cities, the continuing lack of water and electricity, the tendency of American troops to lock themselves up in their fortified quarters except for often brutal operations, had already undermined the presumed sympathy of Iraqis. American ignorance of the Arab world, of its past, of its complexities, of its humiliations, the absence of administrators or military leaders who speak Arabic, have obviously not helped matters. A series of well-known problems has been the result.

The first is the return of the "Vietnam syndrome": once again we find confused objectives, a misunderstanding of the attitude of the "natives" toward the "liberators," confrontations between terrorists of mysterious origins and experience and heavy conventional forces. As in Vietnam, the choice at present is between an "undignified" withdrawal, which remains unacceptable to the hard-liners in the Bush administration, and an increase in foreign military forces, but it is unlikely that anyone is going to join the coalition at this stage, and an increase in American forces would be massively unpopular.

Another familiar problem is the division between the hard-liners, who are still powerful and whose most articulate spokesman, Rumsfeld, is most hostile to such an increase, and those who, in the rather weakened Department of State, would like more help from the members of the U.N. without yielding too much power to the U.N.

Finally, and above all, while the evidence of collusion between Saddam Hussein and al Qaeda was extremely weak, American occupation, which has been fatal for Saddam, has been a splendid occasion for the former supporters of Saddam, for the disciples of bin Laden and some other terrorist groups that have come from different parts of the Arab and Muslim world to infiltrate Iraq, whose huge borders are impossible to seal off. These terrorists have committed and continue to commit murder and sabotage, and opened a second front for the fanatics of suicide bombing. Many Iraqis, happy to be rid of a tyrant, remark that at least he preserved order, and are eager to gain control of their own affairs.

The second conclusion concerns order or, rather, disorder, in today's world. After the end of the cold war, when both camps had, each on its side and by agreement between them, made a certain type of order prevail and preserved global peace through the fear of nuclear annihilation, there was room in fact for only one obviously imperfect but realistic formula for world order. It was an order in which legitimacy and normativity were to be assured by the U.N., i.e., the society of states, with the U.S. as dominant secular force at the service of rules and principles to whose creation it had mightily contributed. This supposed an internationalist America, skillful not only in the use of force but also in the use of "soft power," the capacity to attract and to convince. In resorting to force, such an America would have had to respect the rules of the game and use the institutions which it so largely contributed to creating after 1945, in order to resist aggression, to restore peace in decomposing states, and to build a common policy of nonproliferation. All of this obviously presupposed reinforcing the means at the disposal of those institutions and particularly of the U.N.

This ideal picture has been damaged by two unforeseen factors. The first was the globalization of terrorism, the rise of a nonstate world society of fanatics, nihilists, and the desperadoes and the humiliated of all countries. It had manifested itself long before September 11, but the events of that day revealed the extent to which the phenomenon was both complex in its causes and worldwide in its manifestations. The members of the U.N. are all targets, but they are still divided in their reactions and attitudes.

It would be necessary both to strengthen and to coordinate police controls and to resort to international criminal justice in order to treat the terrorists as pariahs like yesterday's pirates and the authors of crimes against humanity. But the road selected by the United States was that of a declaration of "war" against terrorism, the creation of the notion of "illegal combatants," and the assimilation of states suspected of sheltering terrorists to the terrorists themselves. This was playing into their hands. The second factor is indeed the abandonment by Washington of the role it had so successfully played since 1945, both by choice and by necessity, in the fight against the Soviet Union. This had been a role of cooperation and multilateralism. The temptation of unilateralism, conceived as a manifestation of American exceptionalism, had always been present. But the second Bush administration gave military power a disproportionate preponderance, although even in the fight against terrorism it is only one tool among many others, and although the effectiveness of *power* depends largely on the *authority* of the U.S., of which *legitimacy* is a major component. The administration preferred to treat the allies as a mass of subordinates; it has divided or marginalized those institutions that were not sufficiently docile and resorted to "coalitions of the willing" recruited by Washington, relegated the U.N. to secondary tasks when it became obvious that the U.S. no longer controlled its political organs, and proclaimed the right of the dominant nation to choose among international norms those that suited it. It is as if the terrorists and the state that declared unlimited war on them had colluded to play the role of gravediggers of a very fragile international order which George Bush the father had built.

In the long run, the Americans will return to the policy of cooperation which had been so successful after 1945, and will understand that for two reasons at least imperial America is neither desirable nor possible. The first is the nature of the problems, including the fight against terrorism, or nuclear proliferation, or the misery of a vast part of the third world. All require multilateral action. The decrepitude of many states, and the internal and external conflicts it provokes, particularly require the reinforcement of the U.N. All the arguments that assume (with approval or disapproval) that post-1945, or post-1989, America is an empire, generalize from the elements of military presence and domination in much of the world, and from the global scope and size of American business, which are undeniable. But what is required for a hegemonic U.S. power to be truly imperial: the will to be an empire, and above all the ultimate control of others (through direct rule, or indirect but effective rule) is not very compatible with either America's public mood, or with the present international system, as the collapse of the Soviet empire and the earlier demise of colonial empires have shown. The second reason is the inaptitude of Americans to play an imperial role, a task which requires patience and expertise and a willingness to spend gigantic resources which one does not find in a nation that is still deeply marked by its anticolonial origins and its concentration on domestic problems. But in the short run, the line followed by the Bush administration has been disastrous because it has deprived American power of its legitimacy, and nobody knows how long it will take for a complete return to prudence and a respect for the opinion of other countries. As for the latter, even if they wish for a really multipolar world, they have few chances of reaching it soon. This, however, should not prevent them from behaving as independent countries whose policy is not systematically aligned on America's; they should be capable of taking initiatives, of getting together to act more efficiently and, in the case of the Europeans, they need to be willing and able to transform their union into an association endowed with real political and diplomatic means. It is the only way of influencing American policy and of hastening its most probable evolution.

I have tried in this book to express the real significance of the Iraqi conflict. The bipolar world after 1945 was a confrontation both of might and of legitimacy. Since 1990 the world is unipolar but the "hyperpower" is limited by interdependence, by the capacity of resistance even weak sovereign states have, and by the rise of terrorism. The fundamental choice today is clear. Either the United States will accept, as in the 1990s, that unipolarity is to be asserted in a framework of reciprocal agreements, institutions however imperfect, and universal norms, so as to be able to fight common battles and to diminish resistance to American domination, or else the latter will take the form of an empire founded on military force that seeks its legitimacy in a very unconvincing discourse of universal liberation. That discourse and the use of force, preaching, and the stick, do not go well together. The expedition in Iraq has shown the difficulties of imperial politics.[1]

At present, within what might be called the Establishment, the debate on American foreign policy has been an increasingly tense dialogue between two prescriptions. One is indeed the imperial one, exemplified by the neoconservatives and favored by the great admirer of British imperialism, Prof. Niall Fergusson, who criticizes Americans mainly for not having acknowledged the responsibility of having donned the mantle of imperial control which the British had to let go. On the other side, we find Democrats or policymakers who have served Democratic administrations, who are increasingly unhappy with the consequences of the imperial policy for the reputation of the United States in the world, indeed, for the influence of America, given the need for foreign cooperation and support in almost any area of foreign policy and also the fact that it is only in the military realm that the United States has an overwhelming superiority over others. As Joseph Nye has pointed out, in all the other areas of power, there is no unipolarity. The problem with the second view is that many of those who espouse it still have a grandiose view of America's power and vision. Let us take the example of Zbigniew Brzezinski's new book, *Choice*. What he advocates is extensive consultation with America's allies, a willingness to take their views into account and to take full advantage of the institutions in which the U.S. and they coexist, but at the end of the

1. On these points, see Tzvetan Todorov, *Le nouveau désordre mondial* (Paris: Laffont, 2003).

day, given the unique role of the United States in the world, if there is still disagreement, it is necessary for the United States to set the policy and for its friends and allies to follow. While this is certainly more than just a courteous form of Bushism, it is still somewhat unrealistic. This is a highly complex world in which lesser powers have many ways of opposing American preferences, of obstructing American designs even when, as in the promotion of democracy in the Middle East, these are well intentioned and aim at desirable objectives. What is necessary is not just a kind of period of grace in negotiations before the United States, which in the words of a Democratic foreign minister, Madeleine Albright, "sees farther and is the indispensable nation," lays down the law.

Leadership, which in the second conception of foreign policy is opposed to dictation, the characteristic feature of Bush diplomacy, can cover a multitude of approaches. In addition to that candidly described by Brzezinski, there is another form of leadership which consists in trying to reach a genuine consensus with one's allies and with other concerned countries, depending on the subject matter, and then indeed of using America's multiple forms of power and influence in order to obtain with their help the enforcement of such a consensus. It is true that the United States has many levers at its disposal for leadership, but leadership in democratic societies does not consist merely in the state consulting and then doing pretty much what it wants. There has to be what John Rawls in his approach to liberalism calls an overlapping consensus, which the state then has to reflect and apply in its actions. But we have not reached much awareness of this admittedly subtle difference between two definitions of leadership—ultimate command versus true partnership.

Ultimately, it is only if the United States moves toward this third approach that there is a chance for performing a gigantic task that has been neglected in recent years, that of helping the development of the poorer countries of the world and the poor in many of the countries that now have a prosperous elite presiding over large zones of poverty. As long as this task is neglected, the roots of humiliation and internal trouble, often accompanied by external intervention, will remain deep and, while terrorism has many other, largely political or religious, causes, mass misery certainly contributes to its growth. Equally necessary is the launching of a multifaceted effort of building solid and fair state institutions in crumbling or failed countries. Such tasks certainly exceed the capacity of any single country, but they also require a courageous and dramatic shift from excessive military expenses that correspond more to the needs of defense industries, a futile search for absolute security, and a fascination with new weapons of dubious usefulness than to the threat that we will be facing in the years to come. Such a shift is advocated by no politician in the United States and yet what the use of a budget of $450 billion for defense might be has never been properly answered. Add to this the problems of the environment and the need for the United States to increase and encourage the conservation of oil: a new foreign policy would have to take such requirements into far more serious consideration. The alternative is a world of weak or pseudostates in great number, the most fertile ground for terrorism, with a network of global institutions of limited power and scope, and an arrogant but overstretched superpower whose ambitions and responsibilities far exceed its capacities, and whose self-image is far more flattering than the view from abroad.

There is a third problem, which is too large to be fully dealt with in this book: the United States has been sliding from being an imperfect liberal democracy toward a kind of populist authoritarianism. The history of Europe provides many examples: each one has its specific features; all correspond to moments of distress and disarray. Here, the seizure of power by a type of Republicanism that is not conservative (many conservatives are among the most eloquent critics of "Bushism") but radical, utopian, and imperialist abroad, reactionary and antiliberal within, can be explained: the election of the year 2000, the demoralization of the Democrats that followed, are largely responsible. Above all, Bush has exploited the trauma of September 11, 2001, by playing with virtuosity on the fears of the public, while offering it the flattering vision of an America that is both dominating and exporting universal and democratic values. He has also exploited an ancient and latent Manichaeism in which the United States, at the service of the good, leads the fight against evil. One must furthermore take into account the decline of civic spirit: a mix of indifference toward politics, the success of antistate campaigns, the presentation of tax cuts as a sacred right, all this has diverted the young from the state, led to the degradation of public services, to generalized cynicism toward political life and toward the world of business, to the fact that many citizens, generally the poorest, do not vote, and finally to the domination of Congress by lobbies which block any deep reform of election financing. One also witnesses a growing gap between the rich and the poor, the well educated and the barely educated, which paradoxically provides the volunteer army with a bounty of the poor and barely educated, and thus diverts them from the temptations of class or ethnic warfare (since many of them are Blacks or Latinos) toward an often unquestioning superpatriotism.

In such conditions, a small group of well-financed neoconservatives supported by the most popular media, and a significant and growing force of far-right Christians who defend traditional values, denounce modern mores, and fiercely admire the right wing in Israel, can obtain a disproportionate importance, because they at least have a "vision" to offer. But there is more: there is the disturbing fact, which is not entirely

INDEX